Early Mesopotamia and Iran

MESOPOTAMIA

McGraw-Hill Boo

EARLY

AND IRAN

M. E. L. Mallowan

OMPANY · NEW YORK

DESIGNED AND PRODUCED BY THAMES AND HUDSON

CONTENTS

GENERAL EDITOR'S PREFACE

One of the greatest historical problems is that concerned with the origins of what we today call civilization. Definition is perhaps not easy, but we should surely not be far from the mark if we thought of civilized societies as those which worked out a solution to the problem of living in a relatively permanent community, at a level of technological and social development above that of the hunting band, the family farmstead, the rustic self-sufficient village or the pastoral tribe, and with a capacity for storing information in the form of written documents or their equivalent. Civilization, like all human culture at whatever level, is something artificial and man-made, the result of making tools (physical and conceptual) of increasing complexity in re-. sponse to the enlarging concepts of community life developing in men's minds.

Such development will only present itself as a psychological need in a climate of thought in which innovation is considered desirable by the individual and socially acceptable to the community. Many human societies have achieved an admirable and well-functioning adjustment to their environment, but this once attained, have felt no desire to alter the state of affairs, but rather to conserve their established traditions. Such conserving societies seem to have formed the norm in antiquity, but sporadically there have appeared peoples to whom innovation and change, rather than adherence to tradition, gave satisfaction and release: these innovating societies are those which we can class as the founders of civilization. It is difficult to sustain the thesis that all human societies should have moved towards civilization as an inevitable process; the phenomenon seems almost a sport or freak of development in its initial stages. And in the Old World we have one of these rare manifestations well documented in the Near East, in the Mesopotamian and Iranian area described in this book.

From about 10000 BC in this part of the world a swing in subsistence-economics from hunting and food-gathering to animal and plant domestication had taken place. By the beginning of the fourth millennium BC, when this book opens, a widespread peasant economy, with agriculture at a sufficient level of competence to support permanent villages and even small towns, was characteristic of large areas of the Ancient East. But in Mesopotamia the innovating tradition continued, gathered momentum, and produced the essential background for civilization, the literate city-state.

It becomes an age of cities, their inhabitants as proud of them as were the Greeks of theirs. In the tragic and moving Sumerian epic of Gilgamesh, legendary founder of Uruk, the reader is called upon at the outset of the poem to admire the city and its defences:

'Look at it still today: the outer wall where the cornice runs, it shines with the brilliance of copper; and the inner wall, it has no equal. Touch the threshold, it is ancient . . . Climb upon the wall of Uruk; walk along it, I say; regard the foundation terrace and examine the building; is it not burnt brick and good?'

Within the Sumerian cities such as Uruk the people, 'robust, fleshy, with beaky noses' not only developed the skills and trades of the architect, the sculptor, the metal-worker, the jeweller and all the other attendant craftsmen of an active corporation, but through a learned and astute priesthood and clerisy made decisive steps in social organization and speculative thought, involving the great and cardinal invention of writing.

This discovery that a set of conventional symbols could be constructed whereby human speech or unspoken ideas such as mathematical concepts could be recorded in permanent form was fundamental to all that followed. It seems to have arisen from a state of affairs where commercial transactions were no longer on the simple level of barter between individuals, but with the beginnings of a bureaucracy centred on the temples, were becoming impersonal, large-scale and long-term.

Even if later to be committed to writing, in simpler social situations an imaginative literature, the tales of heroes, the genealogies of chieftains and the dictates of the gods can all be conveyed and transmitted by an oral, word-of-mouth tradition, and were of course so composed and handed down in non-literate antiquity.

From Sumerian into later Babylonian times we can also trace the beginning of mathematical studies, initially practical and concerned on the one hand with accounting and on the other with astronomical observations and computations necessary for the due observance of religious ceremonies. As with our own number systems of today, ultimately derived from antiquity, there were alternative series in use, decimal in business practice and sexagesimal – where 60 units of one kind are written as one of the next higher order – in astronomical and mathematical contexts.

Sumerian art, like its Babylonian and Assyrian successors, shows a phenomenon observable elsewhere (in Egypt or Crete for instance), the development of an interest in the naturalistic representation of the human body and the use of narrative compositions. The dominance of the classical tradition, itself derived from these earlier conventions, has sometimes tended to make people think that such a preoccupation with naturalism, and with man and his actions (or the gods and their doings), an artistic norm, but here again we are encountering a phenomenon closely bound up with other aspects of emergent civilization, and no more inevitable or invariable. An increasing command of control over nature would tend to make men dissociate themselves from the rest of the natural creation and increase self-consciousness and egocentricity which could be commemorated in paint or sculpture. And again, the permanency of the community ('Touch the threshold it is ancient'—the city endures beyond the individual's span) would lead to the concept of the monument to inform and impress posterity; so too writing is essentially the outcome of an historical sense, the preservation of a past, however short, and side-by-side with the records of the scribes would go the narrative or anecdotal scenes of the artists.

Linguistically we move, in the Mesopotamian world of the third millennium BC, from the Sumerian language for which the cuneiform script was first devised, into the Semitic of the Kingdom of Agade and its successors. And by 2000 BC or so we have evidence of barbarian movements soon to affect and afflict this world. At Hissar in the Elburz foothills south of the Caspian Sea the city was sacked in circumstances that may relate to the exploits of those speaking not Semitic, but Indo-European languages, heralds of a new order of things when power will shift to the Aegean and Anatolia under Greeks and Hittites.

STUART PIGGOTT

INTRODUCTION

The essay which I have written in the succeeding pages is a severely compressed account of the archaeological evidence concerning the beginnings of civilized life in Mesopotamia and Iran. Originally written as a chapter in the large volume entitled *The Dawn of Civilization*, it was never intended to be self-contained, but was designed to be considered against a much broader canvas of world archaeology and history. Nevertheless the publishers have thought it worth while to print what was previously written within separate covers, adding generously to the illustrations which must serve as fresh signposts on the road to further discovery of an ancient and glorious stage in man's development. My purpose in writing these few pages has been not to point a moral, but to set before the general reader, and particularly the University student, some elementary information about human achievement in the third millennium BC. The evidence is not easily accessible and may serve to elucidate some of the extensive literature that has already appeared on the subject, often in obscure places.

Oriental archaeology moves apace, and we are still hard at work filling in the gaps and strengthening the foundations of what has already been discovered. Consequently there are new things to describe that have been added to the picture since these pages were first penned. In Mesopotamia, an expedition directed by Dr Lenzen at Warka (ancient Uruk), has discovered a rich deposit of treasure buried within a deep shaft which looked at one time as if it was going to be ancestral to the Royal Graves at Ur. This shaft however turned out to be a place in which burnt offerings, including a few animal remains, had been sacrificed to the gods; it contained beautiful stone vases, pottery, inlaid wooden furniture, and finely made objects of the Jemdet Nasr period that marked it as the finest example yet found of the *opferstätten* so commonly made for the gods at this stage in Mesopotamia – a comparatively modest step in the direction of that terrible human sacrifice that culminated in Ur. The building which contained this deposit was sunk into the ruins of an older temple – known as the 'stone-cone-mosaic' temple and hallowed for eternity the sacred property which the temple had once contained. The mysterious ritual sacrifice which followed after the abandonment of the temple may, according to Dr Lenzen, have been connected with a change in the form of worship at the time.

Nor has epigraphy lagged behind archaeology, for the assiduous labours of Professor S. N. Kramer and his colleagues have not only brought to life a Heroic Age in ancient Sumer, but have revealed from tablets found at Nippur that the hero-kings of mythology were indeed historic figures. We can now be confident that Gilgamesh, a kind of Sumerian Hercules, reigned in the city of Uruk and built its walls a little before the middle of the third millennium B C. The strengthening of the historical structure now enables us to make a case for the archaeological identification of fluviatile deposits at Kish and Shuruppak with Noah's Flood, as I have attempted to prove in *Iraq*, vol. XXVI (1964).

Elsewhere, in Iran, Mr David Stronach, digging at Yarim Tepe not far from the southern shore of the Caspian Sea, on the other side of the mountain from Tepe Hissar, has, thanks to the fortunate discovery of organic material amenable to Carbon 14 dating, confirmed the chronology for Hissar (III B, C,) already offered in these pages; the architecture, metallurgy, and *objets d'art* which go with the famous 'Burned Building' at Hissar may with confidence be assigned to a period not far removed, plus or minus from 2000 B C; and here we now have an assured tie with parallel developments which were going on as far away as Babylonia and Assyria.

But however much new discovery adds to our knowledge annually, both in Iraq and in Iran, we may rest assured that the vital contribution made by the Sumerians to the development of civilized life will remain as one of man's great achievements, for they were the peoples who invented writing and made man civilized. The Sumerians moreover were outstanding in the invention and execution of 'the polite arts', within which I include architecture. I hope that the following pages and accompanying illustrations have made this clear and have helped to show how the Sumerian impact was felt by the more conservative, yet intensely artistic Iran, which had to develop its native genius without the formative influences that the riparian geography of Mesopotamia exercised on its inhabitants.

M.E.L.M.
July, 1964

CHRONOLOGY

The relation in time of the archaeological levels of some of the major sites in Mesopotamia and Iran (after Le Breton). The dates mentioned in the text are based largely on the system which was originally proposed by Professor Sidney Smith whose longer chronology, as opposed to the various shorter schemes offered by other authorities, has been increasingly strengthened by recent evidence. We have therefore adopted the following dates: Hammurabi *acc.* 1792 BC, Sargon of Agade *acc. c.* 2370 BC. Before that time we have to reckon in round numbers, and in our opinion the weight of the archaeological as well as of historical evidence, early synchronisms with Egypt, and the high dating for prehistoric material which has been obtained from C-14 analyses, tend to support the relatively high dates which we have proposed. It will however be some years before we can obtain a sufficient number of C-14 samples both from Early Dynastic sites in Mesopotamia and from Bronze Age settlements in Iran to enable us to arrive at a conclusive chronology.

	PERIOD	SOUTH MESOPOTAMIA				SUSA	NORTH MESOPOTAMIA				IRAN	
		Various sites	UR	ERIDU	URUK (WARKA)		GAWRAH	HASSUNA	NINEVEH	Various sites	SIYALK	GIYAN
2180-1960 BC		Kish	UrDyn. III		Eanna Temple							
2370 BC		L Cem. A Cem. Y	SARGONID				S A R G O N I D					
	E.D. III		Ur Dyn. I Royal Tombs		I	D (II)	VII		Late Seal Impressions			IV ?
	E.D. II								Ninevite V			
	E.D. I				II							
2900 BC	PROTO-LITERATE (d)		Jemdet Nasr		III	C	VIII (a) ? „ (b)			Brak Eye Temple	IV	
	(c)											
	LATE URUK				IV(a) IV(b) V		„ (c) IX		Ninevite IV		?	
	?				VI VII VIII	B						
	EARLY URUK		Ur'Ubaid III		XII XIII XIV	A (I)	XI (a) ? XII XII (a)			Arpachiyah	III	V (d)
3500 BC	LATE 'UBAID	'Uqair	Ur'Ubaid II	VI	XV XVI XVII XVIII	Susiana	XIII		Early Seal Impressions Ninevite III			V (c)
	EARLY 'UBAID	Hajji Muhammad	Ur'Ubaid I	VIII XIII			XV XVI XVII XVIII XIX	XIII XI				
c. 4000 BC												

12

CHAPTER ONE

Urban Development in Uruk and Iran

Geography and Natural Resources

At the stage which is known as the Uruk period cities began to multiply and to expand in many distant parts of Western Asia. This process was already well advanced in about 3500 BC and the most spectacular evidence of it comes from the city of Uruk (Erech of the Old Testament). The site lay on an arm of the southern Euphrates in Sumer, a tract of territory which after 2000 BC was called Babylonia. Here in the middle of the fourth millennium BC art and architecture, many different kinds of technology, and eventually metallurgy, began to display unprecedented developments. Elaborately buttressed walls, lofty temples and public buildings, their façades decorated with a polychrome mosaic of clay cones, greeted the traveller as he passed through the town gates. This was but one of many Mesopotamian townships; Ur, Eridu, Lagash, and Nippur must have presented a similar appearance, and far up the Euphrates places such as Mari and beyond it Brak in the Habur valley showed how far this particular form of urban life had spread.

Such complex organizations were unable to exist without access to many different kinds of raw materials, mostly imported from abroad. Trade, the organization of labour,

Ill. 1

1   A contour plan of the walled city of Uruk (Warka), one of the most
important centres of Sumerian civilization

sustenance of the people, cultivation of the land, required
an elaborate social organization and a bureaucracy capable
of maintaining records of its transactions. The necessity of
establishing title to property, close supervision over the
distribution of goods, the care of rations for all kinds of
workers employed by the state, could not have been
systematically organized in these expanded communities
without the aid of written records. The invention of
writing was therefore indispensable to the concentration
of life in cities, and this accomplishment, which most men
regard as fundamental to civilization, was achieved at this
period. The city of Kish has yielded what is probably the

2, 3   Both sides of a small limestone tablet, found at Kish, and
dating from *c*. 3500 BC. This
tablet shows examples of the
oldest known picture writing
and includes the signs for a
head, hand, foot and for a
threshing sledge and numerals

oldest pictographic tablet and at Uruk itself in the stratum
known as Uruk IV we have the earliest collection of
writing on clay, at first pictorial, then gradually evolving
towards a wedge-shaped (cuneiform) script.

Ills. 2, 3

Mesopotamia, which we define as the tract of territory
controlled by the Euphrates and Tigris rivers, was a
cradle geographically constructed for the growth of urban
life. Towards the southern end of these valleys there were
broad expanses of flat agricultural plains with no natural
obstacles to movement, capable of producing an abundance of food. An assured supply of wheat and barley,
meat, fish and wild fowl from the southern lagoons had
already in the early prehistoric period known as 'Ubaid
caused the population to multiply. Seasonal leisure between one harvest and another; a desire for security; co-
operation for the production of necessities such as
clothing and housing; the natural gregariousness of
family life, had in a city such as Eridu even before
4000 BC attracted a concentration which must have
numbered several thousands of souls. The care of souls
required temples for the well-being of the gods as well as
of men. These developments which came to maturity in
the Uruk period fostered the multiplication of what we
may call luxuries. Man had discovered that he does not
live by bread alone.

Ill. 4

The most striking symptom of luxury is an elaborate
architecture, nowhere better illustrated than in the cities
of the Uruk and immediately succeeding periods. In
examining the transmission and development of architectural design we may see the extent to which industrial

4 Detail from a Sumerian limestone relief showing a cow being milked with her calf standing close by. Dairymen are transferring the milk to larger containers and probably straining it at the same time. The relief formed part of the decoration of a temple at Al 'Ubaid and can be dated to the First Dynasty of Ur, third millennium B C

enterprise was diffused by direct contact between the most distant communities, especially in Mesopotamia. This comparative study will also serve to stress the different pace of development in Iran which, in spite of many artistic and technological achievements, lagged behind its western neighbour owing to its geographical disunity.

Map, p. 130

The contrast between the two countries may at once be appreciated, even from a perfunctory glance at their respective geographies. The great mountain systems of Iran which encompass, especially in the centre, vast and inhospitable desert have encouraged a straggling disunity of ribbon development in the piedmont, and isolated pocket communities on the fertile hill plateau. There is no trunk river to unite one end of the country with the other. Streams flowing down from the mountains die a quick death on the desiccated salt-plains; the distribution of the larger rivers has tended to concentrate homogeneous developments within restricted areas. Moreover, in the mountains and in the foothills intersected by fertile valleys an adequate supply of water from the melting of the snows, from springs and streams, has usually sufficed for the sustenance of relatively small communities with a limited number of mouths to feed. In addition the mountains of Iran are rich in minerals, in stone and in metals. Iranian smiths and stonemasons have had no need to travel far abroad.

In Mesopotamia the geography is entirely different. Here are two great rivers, Euphrates and Tigris, respectively about 1700 and 1200 miles in length from their

sources in Armenia down to the Persian Gulf. Both
rivers have always attracted traffic, more especially along
their banks, and apart from the flood season, upon their
streams. But of the two it is the Euphrates with its lower
banks, less violent floods, facilities for navigation and for
irrigation which has had the greater effect in distributing
and unifying the products of civilization. One of the most
striking proofs of this tendency is, as we shall see below,
the remarkable similarities in the art and architecture of
Brak with that of Uruk eight hundred miles downstream;
well before 3000 BC these two cities must have been in
close touch with one another, whilst on the middle
reaches of the same river the city of Mari shared in all the
technological accomplishments of Sumer. The Euphrates
thoroughfare has indeed been the very life-line of Mesopotamia and its ancient name Uruttu or Urudu, 'copper'
river, signifies its function both as transmitter of the raw
material from the northern hills of Asia Minor, and as the
valley in which the earliest Sumerian smiths worked that
commodity and gained a profitable livelihood from it.
This was a trade route along which from the earliest times
goods travelled on their way back and forth from the
Persian Gulf to the Mediterranean Sea.

The Tigris on the other hand, swift as an arrow, as the
ancient name Idiglat implies, is a more violent, less
predictable river and has tended to disrupt rather than to
unite communications, so that settlements along its upper
reaches show different influences from those farther south.
A settlement such as Tepe Gawrah in the eastern valley of
the upper Tigris has displayed a very different prehistoric

pattern from that familiar in Sumer. But even the Tigris has been subject to the levelling influence of the Mesopotamian plains, for there is a point in the Babylonian bottle-neck at which the two rivers flow no more than thirty miles apart and traffic has crossed and recrossed from one river back to the other. This reach, known from about 2400 BC onwards as Akkad, has often attracted important urban installations, their rulers well aware of its importance as a nodal point for control of north as well as south. Moreover, the conformation of the land farther to the north has also provided natural facilities for trans-Mesopotamian traffic which, already in the Uruk period, may well have bifurcated from Nineveh-on-Tigris overland across to Erbil and Arrapha (Kirkuk) in order to join the Diyala valley route to Akkad. When, as not infrequently happened in prehistoric as in historic times, there was a dichotomy between north and south it was the lower Zab which acted as the upper boundary to a no-man's-land between it and Sumer or Babylonia.

Thus whilst there have been different stresses in geography making in one direction for unity, in another for disunity, it is on the whole the former that has prevailed, in contrast to what we have observed in Iran. Furthermore the deficiency of raw materials in Sumer which forced its cities to seek stone and metal elsewhere could in the end only be satisfactorily relieved by a co-operative effort in which the several cities, despite intermittent warfare, had to collaborate alike for the collection, for the manufacture, and for the distribution of the goods which they required.

It is true that the wars between the city states and the shifting of authority from one dynasty to another as recorded in the ancient Sumerian King List might seem to provide a contrary argument. But the fact that the Sumerians from the earliest times believed that the kingship over the country had to be authorized by the holy city of Nippur is sufficient proof that the importance of an established central authority was recognized. Further, if we follow the course of history we find increasing evidence of the assertion by single city states, Ur, Uruk and the like, of an imperial power which sought to embrace ever wider tracts of territory within their orbit. This process culminated in the twenty-fourth century BC under the rule of the Agade dynasty which for about a century appears to have been dominant over a large part of Mesopotamia whence it exercised a forceful control on the more important trade routes to Syria, Anatolia, and Iran.

The preoccupation with the task of acquiring raw materials from abroad entailed continuous contact with countries on the other side of the mountains. Already in the Uruk period cities we find abundant evidence of imported limestone, basalt, timber, semi-precious stones such as lapis lazuli and carnelian, all obtainable from Iran. We have a record in the literature of the Heroic Age of a dispute between Enmerkar, a King of Sumer, the legendary builder of Uruk, and the lord of Aratta, a city in the Elamite mountains of Iran. The story makes it perfectly clear that the Iranians were trading semi-precious stones against Sumerian wheat and barley, and a dangerous quarrel arose from the failure to negotiate a trade agreement acceptable to both parties.

This very difficult document, which is still not fully understood, is couched in a style much favoured in Sumerian literature; it illustrates a contest of wits between the two parties, each capping the other with a conundrum well in keeping with the quizzical character and strange humour of the Sumerians. However that may be, this early literary reference to grain is of special interest, for ground research has now proved that wheat was cultivated, no doubt in very considerable quantities, in the 'Ubaid as well as the Uruk period, but that later in Early Dynastic times production of that cereal declined owing to excessive irrigation, lack of drainage and consequent salination of the land. Thereafter production of barley increased sharply in proportion to that of wheat because the former crop has a much greater resistance to salt.

Trade between Mesopotamia and Iran had to seek difficult and narrow passes through the mountains. But these were successfully negotiated from the earliest times. The smaller mountain passes in the north were used for trade with Azerbaijan through the district of Amadia, Rowanduz, or Sulaimaniyah. The prehistoric painted pottery known as Ninevite V was, as we shall see, probably introduced from northern Iran to prehistoric Assyria about 3000 B C and was dispersed along these routes. The main highway however was along the famous pass which led up from the Diyala valley through Bisutun, Kermanshah, Hamadan, and on to prehistoric Rhages which lay at the entrance to the way across the Elburz to the sea through the Caspian Gates.

Ill. 5

Contact with Iran was also maintained through the river valleys tributary to the Tigris, especially the Zabs and the Diyala. The upper Zab was also an instrument for the diffusion of Ninevite V pottery between Iraq and Iran, and similarly the Diyala for that of 'Scarlet ware' which has been found at sites such as Moussian and Tepe Ali Abad in Early Dynastic I-II, *c.* 2800 B C and later.

At the southern end of Sumer the extension of the Zagros hills fans outwards in a yet more easterly direction, and this has allowed room for a broad expanse of plain with an uninterrupted run into Susiana. This district of Iran is therefore geographically indistinguishable from the adjacent tract of territory in southern Iraq, and already in the Uruk period there is a striking rapprochement between the arts and crafts of the Sumerian capital cities and those of Susa – markedly noticeable in the types of stamp and cylinder seals which are sometimes identically engraved.

5   Ninevite V pottery. This type of pottery is notable for its rich painted decoration and was probably introduced into prehistoric Assyria along the trade-routes from northern Iran about 3000 B C

Thus there were many channels for communication with Iran which has from the beginning of prehistory seen the invasion and transit of tribes on their way from Central Asia and from India seeking fresh pastures elsewhere. Most important as illustrating this movement is the trans-Caspian route which has intermittently linked the Oxus with the Tigris. The easier way was along the south side of the Elburz Mountains, for sand, swamp and forest impede progress along the South Caspian shore. Archaeological evidence for early caravan trade along this route has come from the excavations at Tepe Hissar where the discovery of large quantities of beads, especially of lapis

6, 7 Good evidence of contact between ancient Mesopotamia and India via Iran is provided by this dark grey steatite bowl. Indian influence may be clearly discerned in the intricate scene which is carved in relief. A typically Indian bull is shown with its hump back, and a curious male figure with long hair and wearing a kilt grasps two sinuous objects, representing running water, which flows in a continuous stream. Further round the bowl another similar male figure stands between two lionesses with their heads turned back towards him. He grasps a serpent in each hand. A further scene, not shown, represents a prostrate bull which is being attacked by a vulture

lazuli, makes it possible to infer that this district must have been a thoroughfare for traffic which passed from the lapis mines of Badakhshan (north Afghanistan) to the Tigris valley. This trade which may have begun at the end of the Uruk period, in what is known as the Jemdet Nasr phase, continued to thrive throughout Early Dynastic times. Evidence for the reception of lapis lazuli in Mesopotamia has been abundantly provided by discoveries at Tepe Gawrah on the upper Tigris and in the lower Euphrates valley. Hissar itself seems also to have been in touch with Baluchistan where the pottery of Rana Ghundai reveals a ceramic connection. In this part of southern Iran we also find evidence of a transit trade between south Mesopotamia and the Indus valley, a process which was perhaps already established at the

and a lion. The combination of water, bulls, snakes and vegetation in the design possibly indicate a rain-making ritual.

The standing bull is reminiscent of the principal motif on a number of Indian seals. The stone used, steatite, is familiar in Baluchistan and a number of vessels from the Royal Cemetery at Ur were fashioned from this material. This bowl dates from *c.* 2700–2500 BC and the motif shown on its resembles that on a fragment of a green stone vase from one of the Sin Temples at Tell Asmar of much the same date

end of the Early Dynastic period (*c.* 2500 BC), and in the course of the next five centuries increased in momentum, seaborne through the Persian Gulf.

The evidence for the links between Mesopotamia and India through Iran is still tenuous, but decorated stone vessels, 'Scarlet ware' pottery, glazed steatite 'Indianesque' seals, as well as copper seals and spiral-headed pins provide undeniable proof of contact. The most distant tracts of overland territory are involved, and such contact implies movement along routes that ran parallel with the Elburz mountains of northern Iran, bifurcating southwards into Baluchistan, as well as trade by sea between the Euphrates and the Indus rivers. In about 2000 BC Bahrein in the Persian Gulf appears to be an important entrepôt for commerce between Mesopotamia and India.

Ills. 6, 7
Ills. 8–10

8–10 Elaborate red and dark brown geometrical designs were used on the shoulders of vases such as *Ill. 9* from Khafajah, in the Diyala valley, *c*. 3200 BC. Four other vases, also from Khafajah (*Ill. 10*), show the development in design and shape from Jemdet Nasr ware of pre 3100 BC, top left example, through its various stages to the later Scarlet ware. After the schematic and geometrical designs of the earlier pottery Scarlet ware begins to include figures and animals. The vase (*Ill. 8*), restored from sherds found at Tell Agrab, is dated *c*. 3100 BC. The design on the body, shown extended above, includes figures having female bodies and curious beaked animal heads with what appear to be horns

The sharp contrast between the physical geography of Mesopotamia and Iran explains the different pace of development in the two countries. Whereas the former was always in need of the raw materials which are indispensable to urban life, and had to adapt its political institutions to its economic needs, the latter, endowed with mountain pastures and with a sufficiency of minerals, lacked the stimuli which induce small communities to coalesce into larger groupings. It follows therefore that especially in architectural progress Mesopotamia took the lead, and that here literacy was more widespread. The mountaineers of Iran, artists to their finger-tips, remained unrivalled in their archaic adherence to colourful design and the humble embellishments of daily life, as is everywhere revealed by their painted potteries, which were a reflection of their tapestries and textiles. It was only in the last stages of the period which we are considering that dynasties from Iran began to aspire to a control of the elaborate and wealthy political structure which had evolved in Mesopotamia.

The Chronology of the Uruk Period

We may now turn to consider the broad achievements of man in this part of the world from the Uruk period onwards, and here we may immediately perceive how far ahead Mesopotamia was, compared with contemporary Iran. Uruk, modern Warka, has given its name to this stage of prehistory because that site more than any other illustrates a development which eventually became characteristic of the whole region. It is marked by an accomplished architecture and by certain forms of ornamentation which are exceptionally easy to recognize.

Ill. 1

The subdivisions of that long period which was probably already in its maturity in about 3500 BC are of interest only to professional archaeologists concerned

with its minutiae. The Uruk site consists of eighteen levels, differentiated by pottery styles. The material succession has been defined by the evidence obtained from a deep sounding in the precincts of the sacred area called E-anna. This pit, about 20 metres in depth, contained within it the accumulated debris of the long period of occupation beginning with the 'Ubaid. Levels XVIII–XIV are marked especially by a characteristic hand-made pottery with dark geometric designs on a light ground. Thereafter this ware began to die out and was succeeded mainly by a monochrome ceramic, wheel-turned, plain drab or buff coloured, and by an increasing number of black, grey and red pots: these varieties of pottery occurred in levels XIV–V. Uruk ware reached its full development in the period known as Uruk IV which also coincided with the climax of architectural development.

Uruk pottery is widespread, especially its latest products, in the southern as well as the northern half of the country, and has been found in abundance both at

Ill. 11

Ills. 12, 13

11   This view shows the ziggurat of E-anna at Uruk from the north-east. The structure has been much denuded but the stairways which led to the higher levels can still be distinguished

12   Painted pottery from tombs at Eridu. Bottom right: a delicately painted cup in early style.

13   Al 'Ubaid pots which were found at the type site of Al 'Ubaid itself. This style of pottery is widespread over much of Mesopotamia and is typical of the latest phase of 'Ubaid pottery which is also represented at Uruk

Carchemish on the upper Euphrates and at Nineveh on the upper Tigris. As time goes on its sharp and angular pottery betrays increasing influence of the metal types which must have served as models for the less expensive clay, and in the next period Uruk III, usually known as 'Jemdet Nasr', there is abundant evidence of metal throughout the country and also of a polychrome red and black ware which however was less widely diffused.

Different labels have been used for the Uruk–Jemdet Nasr succession which is referred to by some archaeologists as 'protoliterate'. But it would be more satisfactory to denominate the whole of this long period as 'Uruk', since that site, so far as we know, contains a homogeneous series of material. This period is sharply differentiated from the Early Dynastic which begins in about 3000 BC and can readily be distinguished from the intervening Jemdet Nasr, the end product of 'Uruk'.

Uruk Pottery

Our knowledge of the earlier stages of the Uruk period is defective and may remain so until subsequent expeditions to Warka are able to uncover the architectural remains which lie most deeply buried there. None the less there are certain articles which are hallmarks of the period, notably very roughly hand-made bowls with bevelled rims which the Germans describe as *glockentöpfe* (bell-shaped pots). They appear to persist throughout all the Uruk phases, become increasingly common towards the end (Jemdet Nasr) and are ubiquitous, for the type occurs not only throughout Sumer and Akkad, Kish, Ur, Lagash (Telloh), Nippur, 'Uqair, but also in the Diyala valley; at Nineveh, at Carchemish, and Hama in Syria, at Susa in Iran, and even at Abydos in Egypt. At Nineveh these vessels were deposited in hundreds; they were usually turned upside down in the soil and contained vegetable matter and are

14 Monochrome, slipped, burnished and plain ware of the Uruk—Jemdet Nasr period, *c.* 3000 BC

thought to have been used to consecrate the soil under building sites. If this hypothesis is correct they served the same purpose as the inscribed Mandaean and Hebrew incantation bowls which in the eighth to tenth centuries AD were prophylactic against demons. Delougaz has however pointed out that these and other vessels fashioned from a soft semi-liquid paste were deliberately manufactured to achieve the maximum of porosity, and that they would have been perfectly adapted for some such domestic purpose as the separation of curds from whey. Even so they could still have provided an appropriate offering to the devil.

Also characteristically Uruk–Jemdet Nasr are cups sometimes adorned with twisted cord-like strap handles, and vessels which were fitted with long tubular spouts which the drinker inserted into his mouth. Towards the end of the period the spouts were conveniently made to droop in order to make drinking easier. Tab and lug handles, often perforated, were also common. The rarity of painted decoration was compensated for by finer vessels with hard slips, sometimes purple, sometimes of a sealing-wax red.

The predominantly monochrome wares of the Uruk period in Mesopotamia are in sharp contrast to the gaily painted fabrics of Iran where a natural conservatism made for a perpetuation of painted designs. In that country the delicate and elegantly painted pottery of Susa, known as Susa A, is a brilliant achievement. It was predominantly a funerary ware deposited with inhumation graves in a cemetery which contained over 2000 burials outside the walls: Susa was already a populous city. Among the rather restricted varieties of shapes, wide open bowls and tall tumblers, sometimes of an almost egg-shell thinness, are outstandingly beautiful products. For whilst the proportions of the vessels are wholly satisfying, the designs, either purely geometric, or geometric abstractions from

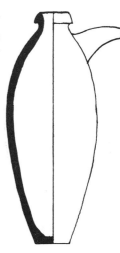

Ill. 14

Ills. 15–17

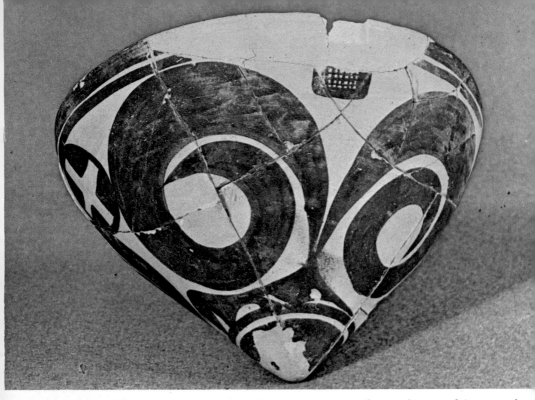

15 Many designs on pottery were sensitively adapted to the form and shape of the pot and are particularly characteristic of the Iranian ware of *c.* 3500 BC. On this example from Persepolis the design is based on ibex horns (*cf. Ill. 16*). Here the horns swelling upwards from four inter-linked ibex at the base of the vase fill the main surface

nature, representing plants and birds, are perfectly distributed over the surface of the vessel and adapted to the form. The broad confident sweep of the painter's brush displays a remarkable dexterity of hand and a sensitive adaptation of design to space unexcelled by any other prehistoric potter. Reeds growing in the marshes and drawings of aquatic birds and turtles remind us of the wet and soggy country in which the city was founded. *Ill. 18* One picture shows a hunter with his bow: hunting dogs, ibex, a member of the horse family, and birds on the wing are portrayed, but always as abstractions from nature, in keeping with the predominantly rectilinear and curvilinear patterns on most of the vessels. Sometimes the design

16 The drawing on this Susa beaker is based on a stylized ibex whose extended horns sweep upwards to encircle a geometric design. The decoration round the rim shows long-necked water birds in a formal, abstract design

17 Susa A beaker, approximately 10½ inches high, from Susa. An elegant, sophisticated, and uncramped sweep of geometric design is combined with a stylized foliage. Early fourth millennium B C

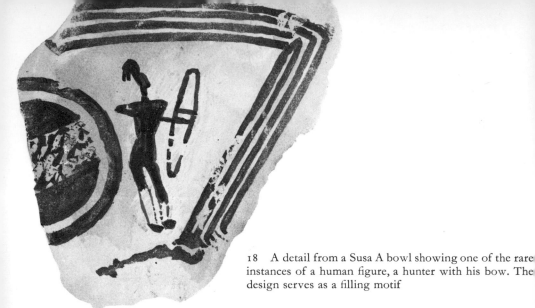

18 A detail from a Susa A bowl showing one of the rare instances of a human figure, a hunter with his bow. The design serves as a filling motif

are organically related to prototypes in basketry or leather; their skeuomorphic character (copying the features appropriate to one substance in another) was long ago stressed by J. L. Myres.

Perhaps the most interesting deduction to be drawn from a study of these designs is that they must also reflect a preoccupation with textiles, and it is safe to conclude that side by side with the pots there must have been woven materials ancestral to the carpets of the present day. The contemporaneity of this pottery with the earlier phase of the Uruk period is proved by its association with stamp seals or seal amulets often animal in form, and that it occurs relatively early in the period has been proved by stratified discoveries at other sites in Susiana where it is intermediate between the preceding 'Ubaid and succeeding undecorated pottery of late Uruk type. It is also important that open cast copper chisels and mirrors were associated with this pottery and that a flat axe was bound in linen, thus attesting the working of flax at this early period. The well-made metal objects are the earliest of their kind in Susiana, though elsewhere, at Siyalk in Central Iran and at Tepe Hissar, the presence of an earlier metallurgy was no doubt due to the siting of these two cities on the early trade routes.

19. 20 Delicately made vessels, almost as skilfully executed as those from Susa, have been found at Bakun in the province of Fars. These pots from about 3500 BC are decorated with abstract designs originally based on nature (*Ill. 19*), birds and animals (*Ill. 20*)

Other Iranian sites of the period can also display fine examples of painted ceramic. Second only to Susa comes Bakun in the province of Fars where again we may see a series of delicately made vessels including fine goblets and *Ills. 19, 20* other types where the painter makes skilful play with counterchanged designs. Once more the artist is constantly abstracting from nature: at Bakun a set of ibex horns is sufficient to indicate the beast itself; horned birds, fish, grotesquely drawn demons, suns, a triangular *Ill. 21* standard on a pedestal, plants, swimming ducks, running water are amongst the painter's repertoire. Well-made vessels in calcite and alabaster, stamp seals, and evidence of a simple flint blade industry were also discovered.

Villages: Bakun, Tepe Hissar and Siyalk

Bakun was a simple village site which consisted of a series of mud-walled houses roughly rectangular in plan. Twelve dwellings could be distinguished with one to seven rooms in each; some rooms were spacious – up to 8·5 by 11·5 metres. The village gives the impression of being an ill-planned agglomeration, a sort of cellular beehive with neighbours living in the closest proximity. There is little evidence of architectural sense here.

Hearths, cooking utensils, rubbing-stones and fire-dogs were found: the basic apparatus of a community living on a primitive agriculture. There were two kilns with separate firing chambers, furnaces and vertical flues for the baking of pottery. However simple the community, it included craftsmen who were highly skilled potters, and at least one of their vessels is closely related in design and technique to the ware of Susa A. Models of painted oxen remind us that these villagers were raising cattle. Little clay models of painted goddesses with prominent breasts, tattooed with swastikas, must have been used for the practice of worship. Finally, evidence for the storage of food, probably cereals, comes from a number of clay sealings which would seem to have been attached to sacks with string.

In other Iranian settlements which may be contemporary with the early stages of the Uruk period we find the same contrast between the squalor of the houses and the elaborate elegance of the pottery. This can be well demonstrated at Tepe Hissar on the southern piedmont of the Elburz Mountains. Irregularly planned and small disjointed rooms bespeak a primitive village, whilst the pottery first hand-made, then wheel-turned, displays the same technological change-over which occurred in the course of the Uruk period in Mesopotamia: the associated circular button seals and square amulets show that there was a certain community of fashion in the cutting of seals throughout northern Mesopotamia and Iran at the same time. Whereas pottery always tended to display strong regional characteristics, the art of the stone-cutter tended to be comparatively uniform.

Similar observations apply to the site of Siyalk in central Iran, one stage of which (towards the end of Siyalk III) is probably contemporary with Uruk. Here again, whilst the pottery is well formed and decorated with attractive designs of ibex and leopard, the architec-

21　Here a geometric design on either side of a grotesque demon figure with monstrous hands throws him forcibly forward as the main motif

ture is disappointing. Nevertheless the buildings are sufficiently solid to suggest that eventually some other Iranian site may reveal a more imposing prehistoric architecture. Indeed there is evidence of heavily buttressed walls which are sometimes niched; another decorative feature is the use of a red ochre wash on wall surfaces: in Siyalk III we find the earliest known Iranian example of a large circular column. The artisans of Siyalk and Hissar, like those of Susa, were already producing simple cast copper tools, daggers, pins, chisels, gravers and the like, which prove that metal, though still rare, was being produced in sufficient quantity.

CHAPTER TWO

The Temples in the Plains

Temple Architecture at Uruk

Ill. 22

When we return to consider contemporary urban developments in Mesopotamia the higher level of achievement as
compared with Iran is remarkable. At Uruk itself (VI–V)
we find the first evidence of buildings on stone foundations. Temple plans were based on those of the preceding
Al 'Ubaid period and display a building tradition already
of a high antiquity. The golden age of architectural
development, however, comes in Uruk IV when there is a
glorious array of temples laid out on magnificent scale.

The normal plan is an oblong building with central
nave, aisles on either side, and podium or altar at the far
short end of the sanctuary. Similar buildings have been
found at 'Uqair, at Khafajah in the Diyala, and at Brak in
the Habur valley. The ornamentation of the façades is
most striking. It consists, especially in Sumer, of a mosaic

Ills. 23, 24

of coloured cones, clay nails, their heads painted black,
red and sometimes white, arranged in patterns on the
wall plaster. Hundreds of thousands of such cones were
used in the adornment of a single building, a most
expensive form of decoration which as excavations have
shown, were constantly liable to collapse. The polychrome
effect must have been very brilliant, and the patterns used

22 Building stone was scarce in Mesopotamia and was chiefly used in the temples for door jamb sockets and foundations. The use of stone as a foundation is an ancient building technique and is illustrated here from a temple at Al 'Ubaid of the First Dynasty of Ur, third millennium BC

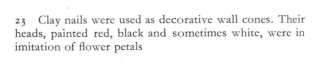

23 Clay nails were used as decorative wall cones. Their heads, painted red, black and sometimes white, were in imitation of flower petals

24 A typical example of wall cone mosaics. The heads of the clay cones were coloured light greenish-yellow and dark blue-black. This example of walling was found *in situ* in a small temple on the western corner of the E-anna precinct, Uruk

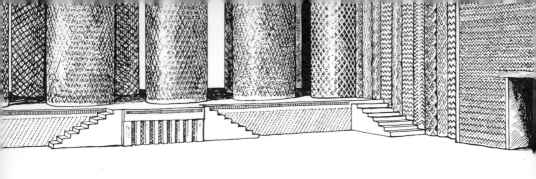

25, 26 The climax of Mesopotamian temple building is reached in the Uruk period and best exemplified in the hall of the Pillar Temple at Uruk. Decorative building columns (*Ill. 26* below) were made by insetting pieces of mother-of-pearl, pink limestone and shell on bitumen around palm logs which formed a stable core. This reconstructed example from Al 'Ubaid dates from the Early Dynastic period, *c.* 2600 B C

seem sometimes to have been copied from matting. It is possible that the technique originally arose from the use of wooden nails which fastened wooden planking to the walls, traces of which have been found on a temple façade at Uruk. The imprint of a wooden stockade was found at Warka on the façade of the north front of the White Temple, and of wooden panelling in the niches. An essential part of the temple décor was an elaborate system of niches and reveals which appear to have been a mark of religious as opposed to secular architecture: this form of decoration, inappropriate to mud-brick because constantly liable to damage, may well have derived from a wooden prototype such as one might expect in more hilly country. Access to the buildings was sometimes through the long side, sometimes through double doors at the short end opposite the altar.

One of the most remarkable buildings of this age is the great complex known as the 'Pillar Temple' at Warka (Uruk). Here the approach is up two flights of steps which confront a raised platform entirely decorated with cone mosaic. After ascending, one then passed through a columned hall in which a double row of free-standing mosaic columns, eight in all, formed an outer portico to the inner building. In addition there were engaged

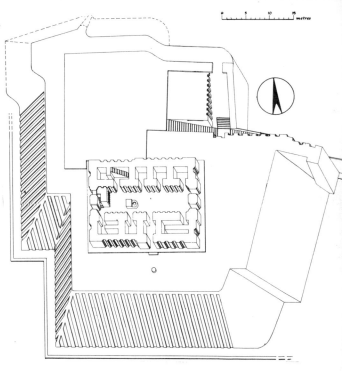

27–29 The Anu ziggurat and
the White Temple at Uruk.
The reconstruction (*Ill. 28*)
shows it seen from above and
the placing of the sanctuary on
the terrace of the temple tower,
Ill. 29 is a reconstructed view
from ground-level. The White
Temple built *c.* 3200–3100 BC
was approached by a steep
flight of stairs and a ramp and is
shown in the reconstruction
(*Ill. 29*) as it may have appeared
at the extreme end of the Uruk
period. Its corners are orienta-
ted to the four cardinal points
of the compass. As each temple
was superseded it was filled in
with mud bricks and its successor built on the foundation thus
made. The temple therefore
stood upon ground consecrated
to the god in perpetuity

columns in one of the side walls. The diameter of these columns is as much as 2·62 metres and is the earliest known instance of columnar architecture on a grand scale. In conception and execution this marks the climax of Urukian architecture: the building is not as yet completely excavated and we are therefore still uncertain as to its plan behind the columned portico.

Many other buildings were erected at Uruk in the course of the same period (Uruk IV); the vast scale of the lay-out at this time is illustrated by a successor to the Pillar Temple known as Temple C, the dimensions of which were over 54×22 metres, built with small prismatic *Riemchen* bricks 16×6×6 cm., a characteristic unit of brick-work which was abandoned in Early Dynastic times. Temple C exhibits the familiar tripartite plan in unusually complicated form, for it appears to be a double temple on a long and a short axis, the two parts at right angles to one another.

The long continuity of this type of architecture at Uruk is illustrated in another part of the site dedicated to the sky-god Anu whose primacy for the Sumerians may be compared to that of Zeus for the Greeks. A building known as the 'White Temple' perched on the summit of a ziggurat forty feet above ground-level, was approached by a steep flight of stairs and a ramp which gave access to the top of the terrace and finally to the temple gates. Here we have the classic form of Sumerian tripartite temple, the prototype of which was first exemplified far back in the 'Ubaid period at Eridu. The 'White Temple' is of mud-brick with white-washed walls; the façade and the nave are decorated with the elaborate buttresses and recesses appropriate to a Sumerian temple. There is a double entrance at the end of the aisle facing the stepped altar or podium opposite. A table for burnt offerings stood in the centre of the aisle and the visitor could leave the temple either at the opposite end to his point of entry, leaving the

Ills. 27–29

Ill. 30

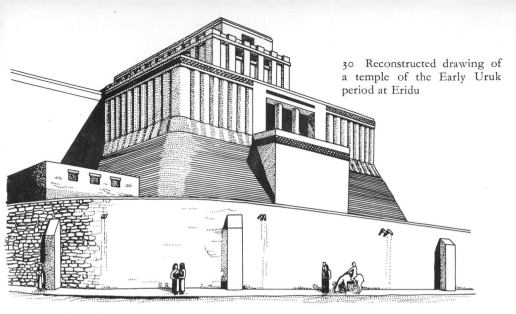

stepped podium on his right, or else through a wide side door. The large chambers on either side of the nave must have been used by the priests both as treasuries and for the storage of ceremonial equipment. There were staircases in the side chambers which gave access to the roof whereon Sumerian ritual prescribed the saying of prayers at sunrise and at other times.

The White Temple was built in the Jemdet Nasr period, that is to say at the extreme end of the Uruk period immediately preceding the Early Dynastic. A round date of about 3200–3100 BC may be assigned to its erection. The so-called Ziggurat or temple tower on which it was set had risen gradually in the course of more than a millennium, for in fact beneath the White Temple the tower incorporated within it a series of much earlier sanctuaries which after serving their time had been filled solid with brickwork and became terraces for later constructions.

The practice of burying the temple and erecting another on the top of it is altogether in accord with the Sumerian concept of the god as landlord and as owner in perpetuity of the ground which had been consecrated to him. Indeed on other sites such as Tell Asmar and Brak, statuary and amulets, the property of the god, were buried

Ills. 31, 33

41

31   The tallest of the statues from Tell Asmar. Because of its height and the symbols carved on ▷
its base, it is believed by some to represent the god Abu himself. The female statue may represent
his consort; the feet and legs of a child are also set into the statue-base

in his abandoned temple, doubtless because they were
considered to be his eternal possessions. This attitude of
mind is corroborated in Sumerian liturgy which prescribed
the pouring of libations, milk and honey over the
foundations of an older temple before its successor was
built, and explains also the remarkable architectural con-
servation which on sacrosanct plots of ground preserved
the essential features of the ground plan for periods as
long as two thousand years.

Other Temple Sites

Many buildings approximately contemporary with the
White Temple have also been found on other Mesopotamian sites. A temple at 'Uqair not far from Babylon is
partly similar in lay-out and of especial interest, because
the temple podium was decorated with polychrome
murals depicting the lion and the leopard, animals which
seem to have been closely associated with divine worship.
Indeed under one corner of the more or less contemporary
White Temple at Uruk the skeletons of a leopard and a
young lion were found buried in a mud-brick box.

   The end phase of the Uruk period through Jemdet
Nasr has also been well illustrated by the series of five
'Sin Temples' at Khafajah in the Diyala valley. Here, as
at Uruk, each building was filled up solid when abandoned. The nave had a podium at one end and in some
cases an offering table in the middle. Whilst there is a
strict conservatism in the lay-out of the sanctuary, in the
course of time, as the gods' domains became richer, the
building grew very considerably in size so that the last in
the series had three courtyards, outbuildings, kitchens
and ovens commensurate with the greater number of
ministrants. As is to be expected, there are many differences in the plan from the more standardized forms of the
Uruk temples: especially noticeable is a long room at the

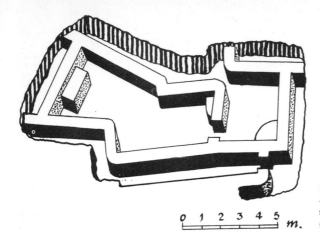

32 The Abu Temple at Tell Asmar is a good example of a smaller type of temple dedicated to a lesser divinity

0 1 2 3 4 5 m.

end of the building usually serving as a staircase, and finally falling into disuse. In course of time therefore the sanctuary, which had once been a central nave, came to be situated at the extreme end of the building and the god became less accessible than he had been before. This tendency towards inaccessibility which coincides with the growth and complexity of social organization is doubtless inevitable both in divine and in human affairs.

It must however be remembered that in addition to the more complex temples there were others of a simpler type, devoted to less important divinities, more in keeping with rustic worship, and these were widespread in Mesopotamia, for example at Nuzi and at Mari. One of the most interesting of these is the earliest shrine of the

Ills. 31–33

Abu Temple at Tell Asmar obviously accommodated to fit in a restricted space among other buildings. It is flanked by a curved alley and has a bent entrance. A small ante-room leads into an oblong sanctuary with re-entrant walls: the altar or podium was placed at the far end against the short wall.

As a last illustration of Jemdet Nasr period architecture

Ills. 34, 35

we may turn to the Eye Temple at Tell Brak, in the Habur valley, 800 miles upstream from Uruk. Here in spite of considerable local differences we have in essence the basic features of a Sumerian temple plan. The building

44

33   This group of votive statuettes was found in a pit beneath the floor of the temple sanctuary during excavation in the Abu Temple at Tell Asmar. They had been piously buried having outlived their usefulness, but once dedicated in the temple they could not be discarded. The tallest figure is 30 inches high and the group dates from the second phase of the Early Dynastic period

is tripartite with a great central nave, podium at the short end, double entrance opposite to it. West of the nave are large storage and service chambers; east of it, a subsidiary sanctuary with narrow and deeply oblong dependent rooms. Large basalt and limestone boulders as well as sun-dried bricks were used in building walls.

A most interesting feature is the cruciform plan towards the end of the nave, a very early anticipation of Christian practice, perhaps so designed for liturgical purposes. Nowhere has the former brilliance of these sanctuaries been more dramatically illustrated, for adhering to the three sides of the podium against the back wall was the

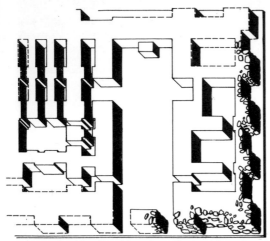
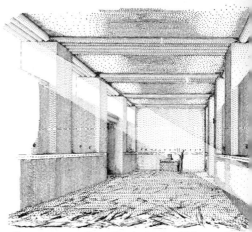

34–36 The Eye Temple at Brak, although 800 miles upstream from Uruk, in the Habur valley still has the basic features of a Sumerian temple plan (*Ill. 34*). The nave is cruciform with a podium or altar at the south end, seen in the reconstruction of the interior (*Ill. 35*) surmounted by an eye-idol. The inner wall of the temple was decorated with rosettes of white marble, black shale and red limestone (*Ill. 36*). This type of cone mosaic decoration achieved a brilliant polychrome effect

Ills. 37, 38

Ill. 36

polychrome façade, composed of gold and of corrugated blue and white limestone. The empanelled front of the podium had been fastened to a wooden backing by means of gold-headed nails with silver stems. The podium itself, three feet high, consisted of miniature prismatic *Riemchen* bricks. The walls of the sanctuary were white-washed and decorated with copper panelling upon which was a repoussé eye-design, the symbol proper to the divinity worshipped at Brak. When the building was finally abandoned it was filled solid with brickwork to make way for yet another temple, the plano-convex bricks of which indicate that it should be assigned not to the Jemdet Nasr but to the Early Dynastic phase.

The Brak Eye Temple exhibited the brilliant polychromy of the Jemdet Nasr period, for the outer face of the north wall was decorated with a coloured cone mosaic and the inner with rosettes of white marble, black shale and red limestone. That the architects of the time were working to certain accepted proportions is proved by the

46

37, 38 A frieze of gold and coloured stones ran around the top of the altar in the Eye Temple at Brak. It is shown in the reconstructed painting of the altar (*Ill. 38*) which is surmounted by an eye- or spectacle-idol based on those found at other sites besides Brak, such as Ur, Mari, and Lagash. The idols vary in size and are made either of stone or terracotta and have a pair of open loops

fact that the nave (18 × 6 metres) is exactly three times as long as it is broad, a canon of measurement which was also used in the temple at 'Uqair and in Sin Temple VI at Tell Asmar.

Cult Objects and Religious Art

Deep down in the artificial platform which supported the Brak Eye Temple there was a series of four older buildings which no doubt conformed to the basic plan of the latest one. Associated with these earlier temples were abundant remains of the treasures dedicated to them. Unique amongst the many thousands of objects discovered in these lower levels are the 'eye-idols' in black and white alabaster of which there are thousands of examples. They consist normally of a thin biscuit-like body surmounted by a pair of eyes in human form once tinted with malachite paint. Most probably they represent dedications by every member of the populace to an all-seeing god who watched over the fortunes of the city. There were moreover many different varieties of idol, including figures with three eyes, pairs with four eyes, and pairs with engravings of smaller idols on the front of the body which were possibly family dedications. More important members of the hierarchy were perhaps represented by figures wearing crowns, one form of which is an attribute of the god Enlil on the much later Kassite boundary stones. A single idol is engraved with a stag, symbol of the Sumerian goddess of childbirth Nin-hur-sag. Its interpretation, like that of the others, must in the absence of written records remain uncertain, and indeed the enigma of these unique objects is one that has long exercised the ingenuity of scholars. There is some satisfaction in reflecting that the true answer may never be known.

It seems likely that these unique idols are to be connected with a simpler form which has been found at other

Ills. 39, 40

39 This unique eye-idol is engraved with a picture of a stag, symbol of Nin-hur-sag, with a bird standing on its back

40 Many thousands of eye-idols were found in the temple at Brak made of black or white alabaster. The thin biscuit-like body is surmounted by a pair of eyes: some examples have more than one pair, others are crowned. The lower right-hand example with two idols superimposed on a larger idol may possibly represent a mother with children

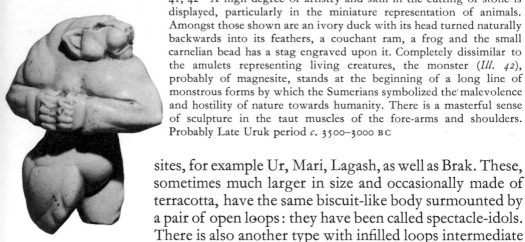

41, 42 A high degree of artistry and skill in the cutting of stone is displayed, particularly in the miniature representation of animals. Amongst those shown are an ivory duck with its head turned naturally backwards into its feathers, a couchant ram, a frog and the small carnelian bead has a stag engraved upon it. Completely dissimilar to the amulets representing living creatures, the monster (*Ill. 42*), probably of magnesite, stands at the beginning of a long line of monstrous forms by which the Sumerians symbolized the malevolence and hostility of nature towards humanity. There is a masterful sense of sculpture in the taut muscles of the fore-arms and shoulders. Probably Late Uruk period *c.* 3500–3000 BC

Ill. 38

sites, for example Ur, Mari, Lagash, as well as Brak. These, sometimes much larger in size and occasionally made of terracotta, have the same biscuit-like body surmounted by a pair of open loops: they have been called spectacle-idols. There is also another type with infilled loops intermediate between these and the eye-idols proper, and this is the reason for seeing a connection between them. In the reconstruction of the Eye Temple sanctuary, the open-looped spectacle-idol has been placed on top of the podium, a reasonable assumption suggested by a small model in soapstone such as have been found at a number of other sites.

43 Downstream from Brak, at Al 'Ubaid, animals were also represented in the temples, but on a much larger scale, and in copper. This relief, 42 inches high, shows the benevolent lion-headed eagle god of Sumerian mythology, Im-dugud. He appears in charge of two stags of the variety *Cervus elaphus maral*, an Anatolian type of stag. The frieze was reconstructed from thousands of fragments and the proportions of the stags' bodies are probably incorrect

44 This figure of a bull was also an ornament of a temple at Al 'Ubaid. It is made of copper originally over a core of wood and bitumen, and dates from the Early Dynastic period *c.* 2600 BC

The amulets discovered at Brak in association with the Eye Temples display another achievement of the same period: a high degree of artistry and skill in the cutting of stone, particularly in the miniature representation of animals. The soft stones such as serpentine, limestone and gypsum, as well as bone and more rarely ivory were most favoured and in them the artists of Brak carved the typical fauna of the country; the animals that roamed both in the plains and in the hills. Lions and other felines, bears, stags, gazelles, monkeys, foxes, hedgehogs and scorpions were the most popular wild animals. In addition there were models of sheep of the domestic and wild

Ills. 41, 42

45, 46 A clay lamb's head from Al 'Ubaid which catches the docile character of the animal. Composite statues are also known such as this bull in grey limestone (*Ill. 46*). The ears and horns and possibly the legs were at one time made of other, probably precious, materials, the eyes and nose were inlaid. Perforations pass lengthwise and vertically through the body and the statue may have carried a religious symbol or a vessel dedicated to the cult

variety, goats, pigs, frogs, eagles and ducks. Usually these amulets were almost in the round, the underside flat and engraved with combinations of birds, snakes and various cryptic signs. Thus was depicted 'every living creature that moveth', to quote the words of the Old Testament account of the Creation in Genesis; and their *Ills. 43, 44* likenesses were deposited in the temple, doubtless in recognition of the dependence of the animal as of the human world on the god's procreative powers. Many of these polished miniatures are, like Chinese jades, a delight to handle. Sometimes the artists made play with the graining of variegated stone and whilst observing a restrained economy of form, contrived to imprison in the stone the living image of the animal. This art was wide- *Ills. 45, 46* spread at Uruk where models of wild and domestic sheep, the divine flocks, were numerous: every capital city of Sumer can display miniatures of the kind, which are also common at the site of Susa in Iran, in association with

47 A little female statuette from Khafajah, the only piece of this type to survive there from Predynastic times, shows a naïve realism and lack of formality which was later lost. This figure is several centuries earlier than the Tell Asmar statues (*Ill. 33*)

48 The stone heads from Brak are important in the history of Mesopotamian sculpture on account of their great antiquity. In this example, of white alabaster, there is already an assurance in the modelling of the face which contrives to express personality and character. The back of the head is flat and grooved and the head-dress is a kind of *tarbush*. Dating from *c.* 3200 BC the head is one of the earliest known examples of north Syrian sculpture

Susa A pottery. But that this is a peculiarly Mesopotamian and not Iranian form of artistry is proved by the fact that on no other Iranian site do any of these models occur.

Sculpture

In larger sculpture too, and in the representation of the human form, the Uruk–Jemdet Nasr artists were already showing considerable ability. The sculptured heads from Brak are amongst the earliest examples of this sculpture. The carving is severely stylized; eyes and ears are primitive in technique, but there is already a sensitivity of facial modelling and an understanding of proportion which achieves a feeling for personality and character. These stone heads were perhaps parts of composite statues the rest of which were of wood, and it may be that the stone models of laced shoes with turned-up toes also belonged to them. It is remarkable that the same type of shoe is still worn by north Syrian peasants today.

Ills. 47, 49

Ill. 48

53

49, 50   A sculptured limestone vase of *c.* 3000 BC from Uruk shows a 'Gilgamesh' type figure grasping and subduing a pair of bull calves. Yet the highest achievement of the Uruk sculptor is represented in the white marble head (*Ill. 50*, right). The simple treatment of planes and economy of modelling typify artistic standards of the end of the Uruk period *c.* 3200–3100 BC and the sensitive rendering of the facial features is not repeated for many centuries. The head must originally have been part of a composite statue, the body of wood, the eyes and eyebrows incrusted and coloured while the hair was no doubt brightly tinted; gold leaf was perhaps applied to the back. The finished, fully dressed statue might well have appeared over-ornate when compared with the pristine simplicity of the head as we now see it

Ill. 50

The highest achievement of this art is however represented by a white marble head from Uruk which in its simple treatment of planes and economy of modelling displays exactly the same technique as that used on the animal amulets, and although unique is altogether in conformity with the artistic standards of the Jemdet Nasr period. The sensitive rendering of the cheeks, mouth and chin is admirable and we have to pass through many centuries of the Early Dynastic period to witness the same skill again.

Two other stone monuments from Uruk possibly even more ancient than this celebrated head may have been

Ill. 51

51 The high relief shown on this boulder of black basalt from Uruk is in the style of the Uruk period. It is part of a stele which was probably once set up in the temple. The costume of the man should be particularly noted, the turban, waistband and long coat which are typical of Babylonia. This can be matched with the carvings on the famous ivory knife handle from Gebel el-Arak in Upper Egypt. The recurved, composite bow is also known from a predynastic Egyptian palette which shows a lion hunt in progress. It is therefore a safe inference, taken together with such other evidence as the mythological beast on the palette of Narmer from Egypt, which is also Mesopotamian, that there was contact between Sumer and Egypt over 5000 years ago

executed in Uruk IV and are also landmarks in the history of sculpture. The first is a large boulder of basalt rock, crudely but expressively carved and no doubt once used as a stele in a temple. It illustrates a hunting scene in which a spearman and archer with recurved bow are shooting down lions. The subject is of especial interest because of certain parallelisms with the art of predynastic Egypt. The costume of the man with turban, long coat and waist-band, typically Babylonian, can be matched on the famous Gebel el-Arak knife handle on which foreign boats also appear as on Uruk seals; a similar type of recurved bow occurs on a predynastic Egyptian lion hunt

52   Also from Uruk the heads of sacred ewes and rams were depicted on this limestone trough. From each of the two doors of the reed hut a lamb emerges. The gate-post has the streamers flying from it which are normally associated with the goddess Inanna

palette now in the British Museum. The inference that there was some contact between Egypt and Sumer at the time is confirmed by the presence in Egypt of Jemdet Nasr type cylinder seals, and indeed towards the end of the period the façades of the first dynasty tombs excavated at Saqqara suggest technical inspiration from the buttressed temples of Mesopotamia where the tradition of niches and reveals was of a much higher antiquity.

A second monument from Uruk is of supreme interest; it is a massive pedestal-based alabaster vase, the surface decorated with a series of registers depicting offerings of cattle and the first fruits of the land to a supreme goddess, doubtless Inanna who is depicted at the summit in front of her two reed standards. Behind her are two lesser divinities mounted on pedestals which rest on the back of a ram: the mounting of divinities on animals was a feature of the much later divine iconography at Yazilikaya in Asia Minor and on some monuments in Assyria, a practice which perhaps ultimately derives from this much more ancient Mesopotamian precedent.

Advancing to meet the goddess is a nude priest who presents to her a magnificent *corbeille de fruits*. Unfortunately the vase is fragmentary at this point, but behind him we can still see the feet and long skirt of a figure which probably represented the king whose

Ill. 53

57

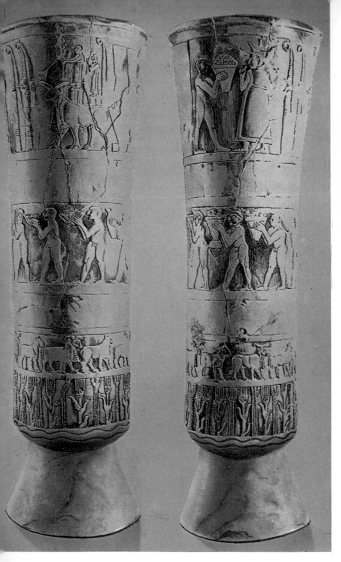

53 A monument of supreme interest from Uruk is a massive pedestal vase over 3 feet high. The design running round it shows the presentation of the first fruits of the land, animal and vegetable, to the goddess, probably Inanna, shown at the top in front of her two reed standards (top right view). On the other side of the vase (top left view) two lesser divinities are mounted on pedestals resting on the back of a ram. The priest, who is ritually nude, advances towards the goddess to present a large bowl of fruit. The figure which stood behind him, probably the king, is only fragmentarily represented by feet and a long skirt, and behind him is a servant in a short tunic carrying his tasselled train. The centre register of the vase shows more nude priests with shaven heads carrying offerings of food and jugs of wine. The lower register is decorated with rams and ewes walking, and wheat and date-palms growing near running water.

The vase was treasured in antiquity as it was at one time repaired with copper rivets. Although found in a Jemdet Nasr period stratum, c. 3200–3100 BC, it may have been made earlier

tasselled train was carried by a servant. In the other registers the nude priests who carry vessels laden with offerings and jugs of wine, the rams, ewes and representations of wheat and the date-palm would seem to indicate that here we have one of the earliest known pictures of the Spring Festival, later on known to the Sumerians as *akîtu* and no doubt already celebrated at Uruk in the fourth millennium BC.

CHAPTER THREE

The Invention of Writing

Architecture, town-planning and the fine arts, the many pictures on stone monuments and on seals of the gods' shrines and of the offerings devoted to them are in themselves sufficient proof of the complex organization of urban life throughout Mesopotamia in the Uruk–Jemdet Nasr period. It is therefore hardly surprising that this was the period during which the art of writing was invented. Coinciding with the great temples of Uruk IV we find the earliest abundant evidence of writing upon clay tablets. The signs were at first pictures of the objects, animate and inanimate, which played a principal part in the life of the community. Sheep ar.d cows, cereals, milk-

Ills. 54, 55

54, 55 Signs were at first pictures of objects, animate and inanimate, drawn on small tablets of clay. These two account tablets date from the Jemdet Nasr period. *Ill. 55* is inscribed in archaic characters derived from pictographs, and relates to accounts of fields and crops

pails, agricultural implements, the façade of a temple, a cattle byre, the human head, the act of eating or drinking, the human foot, the act of walking or going, even the reed standard of the goddess Inanna were obvious pictograms, either isolated or combined, the meaning of which was self-evident. But even in Uruk IV only a limited number of signs is in a true sense pictorial and the significance of many is still unknown. Writing therefore must have begun earlier still and indeed a stone tablet

from Kish, purely pictographic, appears to illustrate the first stages of this art. It is also interesting to reflect that the pictorial concepts which eventually found expression in writing as well as the methods applied were deeply rooted in a prehistoric past. The signs used for star, god, heaven ✳, for water ≈, for earth ⬮, for heaven and the deep ⊞, had long been represented on the painted pottery of Mesopotamia and Iran, and were no doubt already invested with magical prophylactic meaning.

Prehistoric artists had long understood the art of making a part of the object stand for the whole, the principal of *pars pro toto* fundamental to the earliest pictograms and applied for example in the fifth millennium BC by Halaf potters when they designed the

bucranium with a variety of devolutions to stand for an ox.

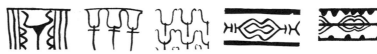

It may also be observed that on pottery this same design was at first represented vertically, just as the earliest scribes tended to favour writing in vertical columns. Later on, when the *bucranium* became a purely geometric stylization it was made to run horizontally round the bowl: similarly the scribe as he drew away from the pictogram towards a developed cuneiform arranged his script in horizontal instead of vertical columns. Since on the earliest texts the scribe began his vertical inscriptions on the right-hand side this change over to horizontal writing had a practical advantage in that subsequent lines were no longer obscured or smudged by the movement of his hand.

Thus the reed which the painter had used for the adornment of his pots was cut anew to serve as a stylus for the scribe. Both conceptually and technically therefore, the development of writing in Mesopotamia presents some interesting analogies with that of painting. On the earliest documents moreover, the arrangement of the signs does not appear to follow any specific or logical order, but seems rather to have been left to the caprice of the writer who, like the pot painter, thus had freedom of choice in the disposition of his subject. It was the tradition of painting, we suspect, that gave the impetus to writing when social conditions required it, and an ingrained habit of mind which stimulated its development. The genius of the Sumerians has the rightful claim to priority for this invention which precedes the different hieroglyphic system used by the Egyptians.

The ideas first expressed in picture writing however were of limited range, and very soon the need was felt and the means found to express more complex messages. To this purpose the monosyllabic tonal Sumerian language readily lent itself; for example the sign TI ($\bigvee$) which depicted an arrow was also the word for life. Consequently on the Jemdet Nasr tablets this sign which had once been a pure pictogram was used as a phonogram in the expression EN.LIL.TI: (may the god) Enlil grant life. Furthermore TI, life, was made to do duty as a syllable in a compound word. In texts from Fara, an Early Dynastic stage of writing later than Jemdet Nasr, the two first phonetically written words were MA.NA, *maneh*, a measure of weight, and DAM.GAR, merchant.

Nevertheless the Sumerians, as Professor Driver has remarked, only took the first halting steps in that direction because their script had been designed to represent their own names for the objects in daily use. Moreover Sumerian words were in the main monosyllabic and were not altered through inflexion, but by prefixed and suffixed syllabic values for which comparatively few signs sufficed. The final development of a syllabic script was in fact only achieved by the Babylonians a thousand years later. The syllabic system was a real convenience to them because theirs, unlike Sumerian, was an inflected language; they were unencumbered by any primitive sign values of their own, and Sumerian monosyllables could therefore be perfectly adapted for this purpose.

Sumerian writing, however, by an ingenious turning of pictures to sound soon achieved a great capacity for expression. The pictogram which originally denoted a concrete object became a symbol for an abstract concept. Thus (✳), an eight-pointed star, was made to signify AN, heaven, sky, and DINGIR, god; it also stood for 'high'. Similarly (𝄖) DU, leg, was conscripted to serve as several verbs; GUB, to stand; GIN, to go; and TUM, to carry off. Such writing was therefore liable to many ambiguities since while in the instances quoted one sign had many sounds (polyphones) there were also conversely homophones such as *sig* which had the same sound and many meanings. In speech the latter difficulty could be overcome if, as we assume, Sumerian like Chinese was a tonal language. In the practice of writing these ambiguities were alleviated by the addition of determinative signs inserted as prefixes and phonetic complements as suffixes, but often only the context can give a clue to the meaning.

Other devices were also used by the early scribes to extend the meanings of their signs. We have already observed the principle by which (≈), a pictogram, Sumerian A, water, also stood for the preposition 'in',

57 Libation jugs of stone were often made in several parts and inlaid with mosaic. The spout of this example from Uruk has been replaced by another found separately. *c.* 3200 BC

58 This stone bowl from the 'Sin Temple' IV at Khafajah has inlay of mother-of-pearl and coloured stone set in bitumen. Jemdet Nasr period

which was represented in speech by the same sound A. The Sumerians also had signs for three other vowels: e, i and u. Furthermore (Υ) the picture of the *mons Veneris* conjoined with the sign for mountains, SAL+KUR, maid of the mountains, was used to signify *geme*, slave-girl, because the Sumerians often abducted their slaves from the mountains. Associated ideas such as LU, man+GAL, great, became LUGAL, king, in the Fara texts which were written towards the end of the Early Dynastic period.

The five or six hundred clay tablets, or fragments of tablets, mostly from Uruk IV, a lesser number from III and a few from II are so far the largest and earliest stratified collection of writing known. It is therefore of singular interest to examine their contents in so far as the often obscure combinations of pictograms and semi-pictograms will allow. The majority of the documents are economic and almost invariably contain numerals which relate to the persons or things recorded in them. Some are ration lists, one in Uruk III is memorandum of the delivery of bread and beer for one day to each of a number of individuals whose names are mentioned, one in each compartment of the tablet. As a rule however it is not possible to offer any specific translation for the agglomeration of signs, but it is clear that they were for the most part lists of commodities supplied to or delivered by officials and others concerned with the administration of the temples. The complexity of administration in 3500 B C required such memoranda and token receipts especially for dairy products, milk and cattle, wheat and barley, and above all for the herds of sheep which must have been one of the most profitable sources of revenue. Indeed in Uruk IV there appear to be no less than thirty-one signs to represent the word UDU, sheep; these no doubt denominated many different breeds, including wool-bearing and fat-tailed, the latter under the sign ($\mathscr{E}$). The tendency to reduce and organize these many variations is shown by the fact that in Uruk III only three and in II only two sets of signs were used for sheep.

Daily Life at Uruk

It is obvious from these lists that fish was an important article of diet; the date palm and the vine also occur. Amongst the domesticated animals we have frequent occurrences of ox, cow, calf, goat and pig, whilst the wild animals include lion, mouflon and deer. There is also a sign for the hound.

Ills. 57, 58 Amongst the objects of daily life we find signs for many different kinds of vessels, vases with and without handles, spouted drinking pots; seed-ploughs, nails, possibly also ploughshares and harrow; weapons include socketed axe, throwing spear, dagger, bow and arrow. There is a sign for a musical instrument: harp or lyre. Boats and carts, four-wheelers and two-wheelers, are common.

59–61 The crescent-shaped Blau Monument is possibly a model of a pottery scraper, and is shown with an actual pottery scraper for comparison from Ur. A bearded figure on one side makes a presentation and a woman faces him across a line of archaic script. On the reverse, workmen are shown beside an anvil, an overseer in the centre

Most interesting is the fact that the sign for copper, *urudu*, is already of frequent occurrence in Uruk IV; it is represented in the form of an ingot (⌂). Nearly all of the above-mentioned articles have assumed the standard forms which were in current use during the Early Dynastic period and occur for example as deposits in the Royal Cemetery of Ur, more than five centuries later. These lists of material objects therefore show that the Sumerian pattern of domestic life had been well established in the Uruk period.

The Uruk lists also contain the names of certain specialized professions. Notable is the NAG.GAR, carpenter, artisan, perhaps one of the oldest craftsmen's names in existence, for it survives today in the Arabic *najjar*. We find priest, SANGA; chief smith, SIMUG-GAL; chief herdsman, SAB-GAL. Of the gods only Inanna is mentioned; EN.LIL occurs at Jemdet Nasr.

A remarkable set of carved stone documents known as the Blau Monuments, once condemned as forgeries, have been rehabilitated through the discoveries at Uruk. They are made of a dark shale (?) inscribed with archaic signs both pictographic and stylized, and as the human figures cut in relief upon them are in the style of those on an alabaster pedestal vase and on the basalt stele from Uruk

Ills. 59–64

Ills. 51, 53

62–64 The Blau Monuments were once thought to be forgeries, but have received recognition as genuine antiquities through discoveries at Uruk. The relief figures on them may be paralleled on the basalt stele and alabaster vase from Uruk (*Ills. 51, 53*). Made of dark shale, their shapes indicate that they are models of craftsmen's tools. This example represents a pointed chisel and an actual example of a copper chisel from the Royal Cemetery at Ur is shown alongside (*Ill. 62*). A standing figure presents an offering of a lamb, whilst below him a kneeling craftsman is shown at work. The reverse is inscribed with a number of archaic pictographic and stylized Sumerian signs whose meaning is still somewhat obscure. The assumption is therefore that they form a record of gifts presented or dedicated to the temple by craftsmen who were attached to it

they may be securely assigned to the period Uruk III–IV. The shape in which the two objects are cut is clear evidence that they are a copy of craftsmen's tools. One of them is a reproduction of a chisel, a type familiar in the Early Dynastic period in the Royal Cemetery of Ur. The other, a crescentic object, is perhaps a copy of a pottery-scraper, for similar tools have been found in terracotta. Moreover, both instruments illustrate craftsmen apparently engaged in making objects on some kind of anvil. On the obverse of the scraper we see a bearded figure in the act of presenting a statue (?) or a pedestal vase, doubtless as a temple offering. The character of the object is uncertain but the top of it may terminate in a lion's head. On the chisel, a standing figure is carrying another offering, this time a lamb. Unfortunately it is impossible to be

65 A foundation tablet from an early Sumerian temple, written in early cuneiform of about 2600 BC. The temple was built by A-an-ne-pad-da, King of Ur and son of Mes-an-ne-pad-da for the Lady of the Mountain, the goddess Nin-hur-sag. She was the goddess of life and fertility

certain of the meaning of the inscription, but since it includes numerals, various receptacles, possibly the sign for fat or oil and for field, we may hazard a guess that it is a record of property or gifts presented or dedicated to the temple by craftsmen attached to it.

Methods of Calculation: Lexical Documents

One of the most marked characteristics of Sumerian civilization is the use of a sexagesimal metric system, evidence for which is abundant both as Uruk and at Jemdet Nasr. Calculations were based on the figure 60, a most practical mathematical standard, because it is exactly divisible by 30, 20, 15, 10, 6, 5, 4, 3 and 2. The number 60 is especially useful as a multiple of the dozen which again is exactly divisible by 4, 3 and 2, and thus

invaluable for domestic allocations of commodities, and
for subdivisions of land. It is curious that side by side
with the sexagesimal, a decimal system was also used, but
at Jemdet Nasr it seems that the latter was particularly
applied to the measurement of barley: its similar applica-
tion at Uruk is therefore probable, and it is perhaps a
legitimate inference that its suitability for cereal measurement was dependent on the tithe as a tenth part of the
produce being payable to the state, that is, to the god who
in the Uruk period must have been the supreme landlord.
The Uruk texts also display familiarity with fractions
which include $\frac{3}{4}$, $\frac{1}{2}$, $\frac{1}{4}$, $\frac{1}{16}$, $\frac{1}{32}$ and $\frac{1}{64}$.

Ills. 54, 55

Thus the early sign lists were made to record an
agricultural and pastoral economy which was based mainly
on the temple's services and requirements. It is probable
that a considerable volume of private business was already
conducted side by side with that of the state: at both Fara
and Ur many documents were found in private houses.

66–69 Foundation tablets are extremely important documents since they not only give the name of the king concerned, but often his father's – hence a chronological sequence may be established.

The foundation brick (*Ill. 66* left) of Enanatum I, *c.* 2450 BC, is inscribed in an early pictographic script. The tablet (*Ill. 67*) written in a semi-pictographic Babylonian script of *c.* 2500 BC records the sinking of a well in the forecourt of the temple of Ningirsu by Eannatum, king of Lagash. Both Eannatum's name and titles and those of his father are given. The clay stamp (*Ill. 68* above) records the restoration of the temple of Sin, the moon-god, by Naram-Sin, *c.* 2280 BC. The reversed inscription, which was in relief on the stamp, was then impressed on the soft bricks before they were fired. Further evolution of the script is shown in the tablet of Ur Nammu, *c.* 2110 BC (*Ill. 69* right)

Ills. 65–69

There is lastly some further remarkable evidence to be gleaned from the texts. A few of them are not commercial but literary, more especially lexical – lists of signs and their values. One from Uruk III is a list of names of fish; another a list of dogs indicated by the sign for UR, comparable to a list of animals from Fara where such lexical texts and sign lists were common. The practice of compiling learned lexical documents, the purpose of which was to organize and systematize every branch of knowledge, is another marked characteristic of Sumerian civilization and it led to as high a degree of accomplishment in the sciences as was possible without using the inductive method, an attainment first accomplished by the Greeks. At all events the discovery of these few documents in Uruk IV is surprising proof that the scientific content of the earliest tablets is directly related to the literary achievements which became widespread throughout the Sumerian capitals from the Fara stage onwards, throughout the third millennium B C. Moreover,

Ill. 70

as soon as writing was invented the profession of the pedagogue was established, together with all those tedious exercises inseparable from a literary education. Behind every modern schoolmaster lies the shade of his first precursor at Uruk.

The Spread of Writing to Iran

The invention of writing was too valuable to remain the monopoly of Sumer and before very long it spread to Iran. Nevertheless, as we have previously explained, the more isolated and self-sufficing character of society in that country did not encourage the diffusion of this art. It was therefore to be expected that the first evidence of a script should appear in Susiana, a land which is geographically an extension of Sumer. At Susa itself at first we have evidence of numerals on clay *bullae* to be followed

70 Before the wedge-shaped cuneiform writing was impressed into the
tablet it was often prepared, as this
example, with ruled lines

shortly afterwards by clay tablets inscribed with proto-
Elamite writing, which is still undeciphered. The signs
were pictograms more or less stylized, distinct from
Mesopotamian and expressed a different language.

The limited use of these early scripts in Iran did not
begin before the Jemdet Nasr period (Uruk III), and
indeed these archaic forms probably survived into the
early part of the third millennium BC contemporary with
the Early Dynastic of Mesopotamia. The same time-lag in
Iran is also apparent in the greater longevity of Mesopotamian forms of design both on stamp and cylinder
seals, which, it is true, show many varieties independent
of the west, but nonetheless are often closely comparable
with types current in the Tigris-Euphrates valley. The
tablets discovered at Siyalk in central Iran are associated
with levels which contain some pot types familiar in the
Tigris-Euphrates valley in Sumer, and others of Ninevite
V variety in Assyria which date from the turn of the
Jemdet Nasr to Early Dynastic I. Thereafter in Iran the
development of writing, for which the evidence is so far
almost exclusively confined to Susiana, followed that of
Mesopotamia.

71

CHAPTER FOUR

The Sumerians and their Contemporaries

At this stage of our inquiry we may well ask the question: when did the Sumerians who played so large a part in laying the foundations of civilization first appear as an identifiable ethnic group? That they were well established in the Jemdet Nasr period we know for certain, since the language of the documents and their methods of calculation are well established as Sumerian. Moreover, since the beginnings of writing in the preceding stage known as Uruk IV are so closely related to that of Jemdet Nasr, it may be taken as virtually certain that they were present in south Babylonia at this stage also. But the question of their identification in this country prior to that must remain doubtful.

Ill. 71

If we follow the pattern of architectural development at Eridu where the basic form of temple plan can be traced back to the very early stages of the 'Ubaid period, we may surmise that the Sumerians were present in the country long before they can first be attested by their written documents. On the other hand if we consider the striking innovations of the Uruk period: the use of polychrome cone mosaic in the walls; the sudden increase of metallurgy; and the marked changes in the character of the pottery as well as some changes in burial customs, we may be tempted to attribute such innovations to the entry

71 The sacred herd belonging to a temple is shown emerging from a byre on this impression a cylinder seal from Khafajah of the Jemdet Nasr period

of a new people: to the Sumerians themselves, whose characteristic appearance on the monuments, robust, fleshy, with beaky noses, is first apparent on the Uruk vase and contemporary cylinder seals. But their broad-headed appearance when represented as shaven and shorn is strangely at variance with evidence from the actual skulls which are predominantly dolicocephalic (long-headed).

So far the examination of skeletal remains has not been decisive, for there is a long-headed type from the beginning with some broad heads at Kish. At Ur in the Early Dynastic period when Sumerians were dominant there was evidence of a long and narrow-headed type. Two of the royal skeletons were said to have been the remains of persons of fine physique and rich brain endowment. With the advent of dynasties speaking a Semitic language (Akkadian) about the middle of the third millennium BC occurs a striking bronze portrait head, perhaps Sargon of Agade himself, who would pass as a typical Semitic sheikh of the desert, apparently long-headed, with high cheek-bones, slightly aquiline nose, fleshy lips and downy moustache. In Iran the evidence from Siyalk, Hissar and other sites is that in the early periods long heads were dominant, although some moderately broad-headed types were already present at Siyalk long before the Early Dynastic period.

Since some of the ancient city names are neither Sumerian nor Semitic it may be that the ancestors of the Sumerians together with peoples speaking Semitic and

Ill. 74

72, 73　Running goats turn their heads and appear in perpetual motion round the cylinder. Their horns are artistically elongated and add to the charm of the design. *c.* 2800 BC. *Ill. 73*, an heraldic group, is composed round a sacred tree which surmounts a mountain. A bull-man and a bull-hero each grasp the tail of a rampant bull and dispatch it with a dagger thrust. *c.* 2300 BC

other languages were present from the very beginning. They came to maturity in the Uruk period about 3500 BC and were politically dominant for a thousand years thereafter in Babylonia.

With the Sumerian period of hegemony we may associate an acute sense of hierarchic property and ownership, the traces of which are manifest in the use of the *Ills. 72, 73* cylinder seal for registering documents. In the engravings of those seals we find a brilliant formal art which in Uruk IV had attained a remarkable ability in the representation of animals, verging on realism, a fine sense of spacing and proportion and a vivid convention in the *Ills. 75–82* representation of scenes connected with the worship of the gods, the dedication of men and animals to the temples. In the Jemdet Nasr period there was a tendency on the seals to scamp the older generously spaced designs and to indulge in a kind of conventionalized shorthand, a degeneration from the free bounty of the older style. This glyptic art was to reassert itself however in the succeeding periods and perhaps attained its apogee in the third Early Dynastic and Sargonid age. In Iran, which favoured the stamp seal rather than the cylinder, a more restricted spacing had favoured a shorthand style from the beginning and the successive changes in glyptic are less violently apparent, except at sites such as Susa where there was often close contact with Sumer.

74　A partly hollow cast head which may represent Sargon of Agade, *c.* 2370 BC, found at Nineveh (modern Kuyunjik), shows him as a long-headed, typical sheikh of the desert, with slightly aquiline nose, high cheek-bones and downy moustache above fleshy lips

75   *c.* 3300 B C or earlier. A king or priest holds sacred rosettes towards long-eared sheep with the standards of the goddess Inanna represented behind him (*cf. Ills. 45, 52*)

76   *c.* 3200 B C. A continuous frieze of a horned antelope amid vegetation

77   *c.* 3000 B C. The horns of the resting antelopes have been extended to fill the space behind him (*cf. Ills. 45, 52*)

78   *c.* 2700 B C. A bearded hero wearing an ornate ball-headed comb holds a pair of rampant bulls by their necks and a bull-headed man to the right stands full-face and grasps two lions, whilst a second bull-headed man to the left, looking over his shoulder, has seized the fore-paw of a lion with both hands

79 *c.* 2100-2000 B C. A presentation scene. The dwarf behind the throne and the monkey above him clinging to a stick should be noted. The crescent symbol is that of the moon-god Sin

80 *c.* 2050 B C. A goddess wearing a high horned hat introduces a worshipper to a bearded and enthroned god. Behind the worshipper a similar goddess raises her hands before her

31 *c.* 2000–1900 B C. A worshipper is presented by a goddess to a god who greets him from his throne. A flaw in the stone has disfigured the god

32 *c.* 2000–1900 B C. A seated god receives a worshipper presented by a goddess. Between them is represented a squat dwarf. The engraving is of inferior quality and the figures are badly executed

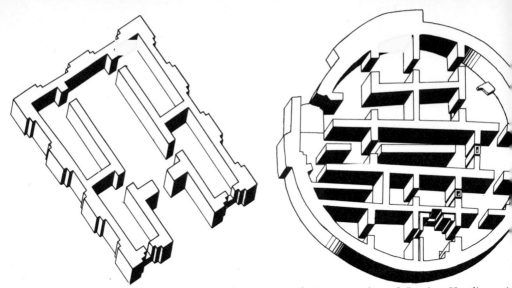

83, 84 Possible influence from the hill country of Mesopotamia and Iranian Kurdistan i
shown in the architecture of Temple VIII C at Tepe Gawrah which has a deep porch at the
entrance. It was probably built prior to 3200 B C: an earlier form of this architecture occurs in
the preceding stratum XI at the site. Another architectural form which enjoyed long continuity
was the round house. The example *c.* 3500 B C from level XIA at Tepe Gawrah (*Ill. 84*), obviousl
the headman's house, was placed in a dominating position and with an eye to defence

Architecture outside Sumer : Tepe Gawrah

We may now consider architecture in places outside th
range of direct Sumerian influence. Some interesting
variations occur at a site such as Tepe Gawrah fourteer
miles east of the Tigris, not far from Nineveh. Here ir
the Uruk–Jemdet Nasr periods we find, it is true, the
tripartite temple plan with central nave and façade
ornamented with niches and reveals comparable to the
architecture of Eridu. But at Gawrah there is one differen
feature which perhaps betrays influences from the hil
country of Mesopotamia and Iranian Kurdistan: it is the
lay-out of a deep porch at the entrance to the temple in th
short side, well-illustrated for example in Gawrah VIII C
an architectural form which seems to make its firs
appearance in a preceding stratum (XI) which was pro
bably contemporary with an early Uruk phase.

Ill. 83

85 A remarkable example of metal work of the Uruk period, *c.* 3200 BC, is the electrum wolf's head from Tepe Gawrah. The teeth are made of gold wire, the ears and jaw separately attached by copper and electrum pins. Bitumen was used to fill the interior of the head and the eye sockets

Earlier still we have another architectural form which in northern Mesopotamia has enjoyed an extraordinary continuity, namely the round house as at Gawrah XI A centrally placed and dominating the site. This was clearly the headman's house; it contained a spacious central hall 13 × 2·6 metres in dimensions, with a long clay partition running down the middle of the room; one of the smaller rooms (E) with inner buttresses originally built with a niche in the end wall may have been used as a sanctuary. The round house had a very solidly built perimeter and was approached by a steep ramp; it was clearly designed with an eye to defence. Around it were smaller irregularly built rectangular houses, the majority very ill-planned.

Ills. 84, 92

The Uruk–Jemdet Nasr period at Gawrah was an extraordinarily prosperous one, and the evidence shows that the whole of Mesopotamia, including cities altogether outside the domain of Sumer, were flourishing at the time. This age of technological progress had made for widespread material wealth, abundantly illustrated by the rich deposits in graves found under the houses on the citadel; stone as well as mud-brick and timber was used in their construction, some of the vaults were corbelled. The dead were buried within the walls, for apparently the

79

86 Examples of gold jewellery from a tomb at Tepe Gawrah, post 3000 BC. The large gold rosette would have been used as a head ornament or sewn on clothing

inhabitants lived in fear of attack and it was desirable for the wealthier dead to be under the protection of the living. Their tombs would have been well worth rifling.

Jewellery and Ornaments

Perhaps the most extraordinary feature of the deposits assigned to the dead is the quantity of beads. One tomb contained 3000; another included 750 cowries which must ultimately have come from the Indian Ocean, perhaps through the Persian Gulf. Among the materials used for beads and amulets there was lapis lazuli, ivory, turquoise, jadeite, carnelian, haematite, obsidian, quartz, diorite and faience. Many of the stones must have been imported from Persia, others may have come from Armenia. The 450 lapis lazuli beads in one of the graves no doubt originated in distant Badakhshan. It seems probable that Tepe Hissar, a piedmont site in northern Iran, was a station on the transit route for the lapis trade, since lapis lazuli beads appear there from about the end of the Jemdet Nasr period and subsequently. This much prized stone was exported to Ur and deposited in great quantities in graves of the second and third Early Dynastic periods, after which time the richer veins may have been worked out, for the supply decreased thereafter.

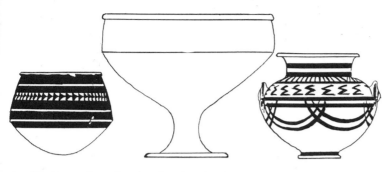
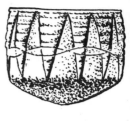
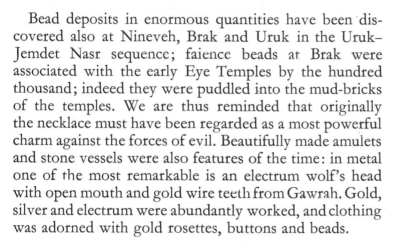

87, 88 Examples of painted Ninevite V pottery and an unpainted pedestal vase. *Ill. 88.* Two incised bowls in greenish clay from Chagar Bazar, the upper example is bound with strands of silver wire. These were cheap substitutes for the more expensive silver ones

Bead deposits in enormous quantities have been discovered also at Nineveh, Brak and Uruk in the Uruk–Jemdet Nasr sequence; faience beads at Brak were associated with the early Eye Temples by the hundred thousand; indeed they were puddled into the mud-bricks of the temples. We are thus reminded that originally the necklace must have been regarded as a most powerful charm against the forces of evil. Beautifully made amulets and stone vessels were also features of the time: in metal one of the most remarkable is an electrum wolf's head *Ill. 85* with open mouth and gold wire teeth from Gawrah. Gold, silver and electrum were abundantly worked, and clothing was adorned with gold rosettes, buttons and beads. *Ill. 86*

Pottery

Towards the beginning of the Early Dynastic period fine specimens of incised grey and black pottery of a type known as Ninevite V were sometimes bound with strands of silver wire, and indeed some of these vessels were probably substitutes for the more expensive silver. Good specimens of such pots have been found in the Habur valley at Chagar Bazar, at Nineveh and elsewhere. *Ills. 87, 88* Preceding this incised ware is a painted variety of Ninevite V which includes bowls and vessels with high

89 Wheel-turned painted pottery from Jemdet Nasr. Polychrome geometric designs in black and red paint are characteristic of the period, the shapes often derived from metal

Ill. 89

pedestals; the latter are often decorated with horned animals which have long giraffe-like necks and remind us of the strange beasts which occasionally figure on contemporary protodynastic Egyptian stone palettes. This pottery, often executed in a violet, almost plum-red paint, is the northern equivalent of the southern Jemdet Nasr ware. It seems that the painted Ninevite V abundant in the Khosr valley of prehistoric Assyria was introduced from Persia, probably through Azerbaijan where it has been found, for example,. on the site of Hasanlu. Varieties of the ware also appear at other Persian sites, notably Hissar and Siyalk where its early context and derivation from even more ancient ceramic proves its ultimate Iranian origin. When it appears in north Mesopotamia and in Assyria it is closely associated with a good quality of metal work, especially with copper tools such as chisels which were apparently cast in an open mould.

CHAPTER FIVE

The Early Dynastic Period
and the Death-pits at Ur

Enough has been said and illustrated to demonstrate that the foundations of civilization had been well and truly laid in the Uruk–Jemdet Nasr period, and to show how large a part the Sumerians played in that achievement which in time spread over wide tracts of north Mesopotamia, Syria, and Iran far beyond their primary orbit. It would require yet another even longer chapter to show how the superstructure was built upon those foundations; but a few landmarks may suffice to indicate the trends of development and to illustrate the importance of recent evidence in the assessment of chronology.

Architecture

In architecture the most characteristic criterion of the Early Dynastic period is the use of the cushion-shaped plano-convex brick. In the northern tract of Mesopotamia however the plano-convex brick was more rarely used. It occurs at Brak in the upper Habur valley, but is not at home on the upper Tigris. During the earliest stage of the Early Dynastic there are Early Dynastic I buildings in which the older *Riemchen* are used in conjunction with the newer cushion-shaped bricks, e.g. in the shrine of the Abu Temple at Tell Asmar contemporary with Uruk I. Why this inconvenient unit of building was employed is

90, 91　An aerial view of the excavations at the site of Khafajah in the Diyala valley. The reconstructed drawing of the 'Temple Oval' (*Ill. 91* right) shows the sanctuary set on an elevated platform with the priests' house located between the inner and outer perimeter walls

unknown; some authorities believe that it was a transition to mud-bricks by new peoples accustomed to building in stone. In fact there is a precedent in Sumer itself where cushion-shaped cement bricks have been found at a much earlier period. It may be that some convention dictated by religious authority was responsible for the perpetuation of this inconvenience in Early Dynastic times.

Ill. 90

The Early Dynastic sequence has been divided into three stages, I–III, and is best illustrated at the site of Khafajah in the Diyala valley where five consecutively built 'Sin Temples' (VI–X) have revealed a remarkable continuity in the architecture. Here was a series of enormous mud-brick temples defended by powerful walls which still incorporated within them the established form of oblong sanctuary. All the necessary service rooms were grouped around a vast squarish courtyard which had now assumed the form that became characteristic in Babylonia after 2000 BC. This stratified evidence is of special importance because of the great depth of accumulated debris embraced by these sequent buildings, each of which was powerfully built and capable of lasting for a long space of time. The many changes of style in the objects associated with them must also imply protracted stages of development. In our opinion a span of rather

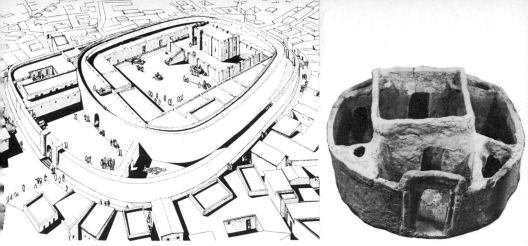

92 A baked clay model of a typical 'round house' from Mari representing a headman's house (*cf. Ill. 84*). It is an architectural model of great rarity, *c.* 2900–2460 BC, and was found beneath a street with a group of pottery vessels

more than 500 years from about 3000–2450 BC is a modest computation for the length of the whole period, and accords better with the long chronologies which C-14 is now indicating for previous prehistoric stages than any of the reductions proposed by authorities who favour the scaling down of Early Dynastic and historic dates.

Our knowledge of Early Dynastic I period is relatively defective in comparison with the abundant evidence for the two succeeding stages, II–III, and it is probable that this was the shortest of the three. It is however certain that the architectural developments characteristic of II–III were already fully established in Early Dynastic I and this is nowhere better illustrated than in the spacious and elaborately built 'Sin Temples' VI–VII.

From evidence at Tell Asmar in the Diyala valley it would also seem that the type of private house characteristic of Babylonia after 2000 BC was already defined at least in embryo a thousand years earlier. The pivotal feature was a central room with flat roof to which the remaining apartments were subsidiary: it was only in the later Akkadian period that this developed into an open courtyard. The houses had only a single storey; small squarish open windows perhaps protected with wooden grilles were already known; they could be blocked with

Ill. 92

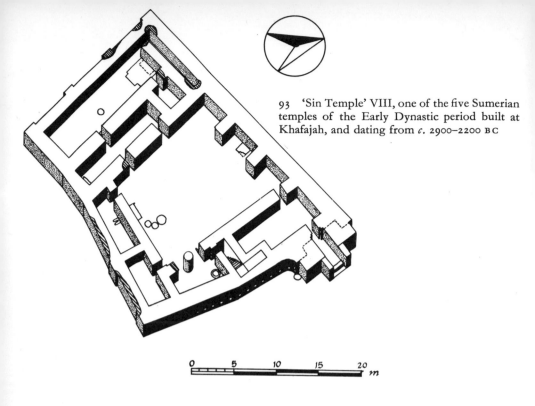

93 'Sin Temple' VIII, one of the five Sumerian temples of the Early Dynastic period built at Khafajah, and dating from *c.* 2900–2200 BC

0	5	10	15	20

m

bricks in case of inclement weather. Cylinder seals with designs in what is termed the 'brocade' style are the best criterion of Early Dynastic I and some examples were found in the 'Sin Temples' VI–VII.

Ill. 91

At Khafajah the most impressive monument of the Early Dynastic II–III period is a sacred perimeter known as the 'Temple Oval' secluding the temple itself from the simple houses which cluster around it. This was a self-sufficient unit which covered an area of more than three hectares including enclosure walls, huge courtyard, workshops and magazines, sanctuary at one end, priest's house at the other.

Ill. 93

Ill. 94

Very important in the Early Dynastic series is a building at Khafajah known as 'Sin Temple' VIII (Early Dynastic II), because of its architectural similarity to a great palace at Kish: plano-convex bricks were the standard unit of construction in each case. The stepped approach flanked by towers; the niches in the façade; and the use of the

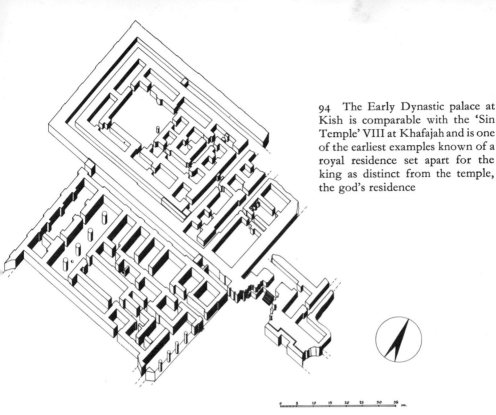

94 The Early Dynastic palace at Kish is comparable with the 'Sin Temple' VIII at Khafajah and is one of the earliest examples known of a royal residence set apart for the king as distinct from the temple, the god's residence

column in both buildings prove that they cannot be very far removed in time, while the objects found in Sin VIII indicate that it is perhaps contemporary with the earlier part of the Royal Cemetery of Ur. This contemporaneity is also suggested by the fact that a cemetery, known as Kish A (E.D. III), was dug into the ruins of the (E.D. II) Kish Palace when it was abandoned, and that the contents of Kish A match many of those at Ur in E.D. III. The earlier sequence is demonstrated by the discovery of an older inscribed tablet embedded in a bench within the Kish Palace, of the pre-Fara type (that is, prior to E.D. III) while the earliest graves of the Ur Royal Cemetery similarly were dug into houses which contained Fara (E.D. III) type tablets.

The Kish Palace and another spacious building at Eridu also probably of Early Dynastic II are in fact the earliest examples known to us of a royal residence set apart for the king. Indeed in the long history of Sumerian architectural development there is no evidence before that period of a separate palace. The architectural evidence accords with that of the texts, namely that originally the king and the chief priest were one. The old Sumerian title *ensi* probably meant the lord who established the foundation of a temple, and it was the temple which originally owned all the land.

The king as priest had special quarters in the temple, the GIG.PAR, and a building recently excavated at Nippur perhaps illustrates separate domestic quarters within the temple complex. Enmerkar, the king who built Erech, received emissaries from Iran in the *gu-en-na*, the throne-room of the temple. We have to wait for a prince of Lagash named Entemena *c.* 2400 BC (end of Early Dynastic III) to find a deed of sale which records that 'in those days Entemena was prince of the city of Lagash and Enentarzi was priest of Ningirsu'. Here we have the first evidence of separation between church and state.

Two generations later, Urukagina was engaged in correcting the abuses which had arisen from the increasingly bureaucratic state with its tempting opportunities for peculation in land, oppressive dues and taxes, and exorbitant burial fees.

When we are able to observe a well defined example of a palace we may assume that the king was the *lu-gal* (great man) and that he lived in the *e-gal* (great house): as head of the state he was still the *ensi*.

Moreover, Sidney Smith has rightly called attention to the fact that since the late Babylonian equivalent of this word was applied to the holders of allotments of state territory won by conquest, it may be deduced that the original meaning implied that the *ensi* was the tenant farmer of the god. And this in effect the earliest rulers of Uruk must have been, as we may judge from the predominantly agricultural and pastoral economy to which so many of its monuments and remains bear witness.

95 The great death-pit of Ur during excavation of the gold objects found by Sir Leonard Woolley

96 A pen drawing of the great death-pit of Ur, which shows the arrangement of the bodies and also bull-headed lyres to the left

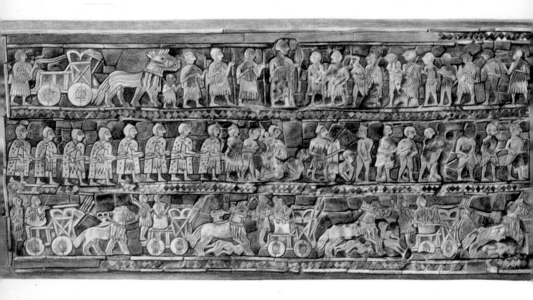

97–100 The 'Royal Standard' of Ur illustrates the activities of the king and his court in peace and in war. It is an oblong box, tapering towards the top and about 18 inches long. The figures are composed of shell and some limestone pieces against a background of blue lapis lazuli. The whole composition was fastened to a wooden backing by bitumen. The 'Standard' was found in a plundered corbel-vaulted stone tomb, one of the earliest in the Royal Cemetery. Skilfully excavated by Sir Leonard Woolley who lifted the panels, they were reset with a minimum of restoration.

The two long panels represent War and Peace and are to be read according to Sumerian convention from the bottom upwards. In the lower register of the 'War' side, the *coup de grâce* is given to a defeated enemy by heavy four-wheeled chariots with solid wheels, drawn by wild asses or onagers (*cf. Ill. 110*). The middle register shows prisoners of war being driven by the king's heavy shock-troops—a 'phalanx' equipped with short spears, felt cloaks and helmets which are possibly of leather. In the upper register the king, who is the large central figure, has alighted from his chariot and

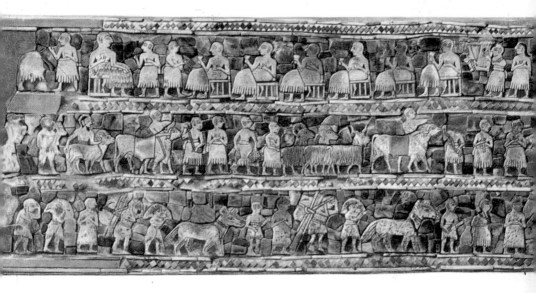

is receiving the captives, who are led in by
light troops.

The lower register of the 'Peace' side
shows servants leading onagers and
others carrying heavy bundles strapped
around their heads in the manner of
Kurdish porters. The middle register
shows bullocks, fleecy rams and possibly
an oryx being led by servants, and a
figure in the middle carries fish. In the
upper register a court banquet is in
progress and the king and his courtiers
drink wine to the accompaniment of
music. The lyre which the musician holds
on the right is similar to the bull-headed
lyres found in other tombs at Ur (*cf. Ills.
103, 105*). The end pieces are composed
of similar inlaid scenes with human beings
and mythological animals.

In all probability, the 'Standard' was
the sounding board of a musical instrument rather than a standard in the accepted
sense since it has no parallel as such in
Sumerian art. Its shape resembles that of
lyres from other royal tombs and the
strings and cross-pieces overlaid with
precious metal were doubtless removed
by the robbers who plundered the tomb
in which it was found. A date *c.* 2700 B C
may be assigned to it.

101–105 The golden ram (*Ill. 101*) and the three lyres (*Ill. 102*) found crushed prior to excavation in the great death-pit at Ur by Woolley. In the left-hand side of the picture bulls' heads can be seen on the front of the two lyres. In *Ill. 103* the bull's head surmounting the lyre is seen in profile, attached to the sounding box inlaid with mosaic. The head consists of gold leaf on a wooden core, save for the eyes, and the bull appears to have a reign ring across his nose. The inlaid plaques below the head represent mythological figures. *Ill. 104*, often referred to as the 'Ram caught in a thicket', is a figure of a he-goat, one of a pair, from the great death-pit. It is made of gold, silver, lapis lazuli, shell and red limestone, and is represented with its forelegs hobbled to the branches of a golden tree. The white shell fleece was fixed on to a wooden body with bitumen. *Ill. 105*, a gold bull's head from a lyre, has the hair and beard made of lapis lazuli and the rest of the head is decorated with gold leaf overlaid on a wooden core

106 The skeletons of the courtiers destined to follow the king into the next world were found crushed flat by the weight of the earth (*cf. Ill. 96*) and the skulls in particular suffered. Careful excavation enabled reconstructions of the ornamental head-dresses and jewellery to be made with accuracy

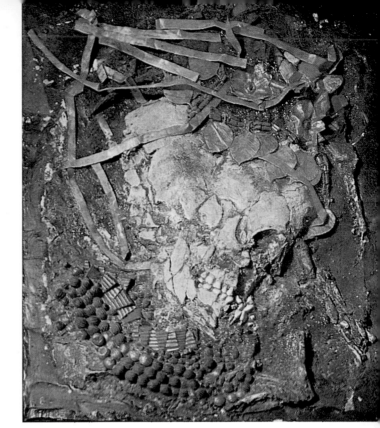

107 Crushed skull of a female attendant wearing a head-dress and jewellery similar to the one illustrated opposite and as found *in situ*

108 Reconstructed jewellery originally found on a crushed skull similar to the one illustrated above

109, 110 Silver reign-rings from the death-pits at Ur. *Ill. 109* is surmounted by a figure of a bull, *Ill. 110* by a figure of an onager. The rein-ring is cast in silver and the onager in electrum and came from the tomb of Queen Shub-ad. It belonged to the Queen's carriage, which was drawn by two onagers and stood near the entrance to the grave

Art, Early Dynastic II-III

The Early Dynastic II–III period is not only abundantly attested by the architecture, but also by the contents of the remarkable tombs of the Kish Y cemetery and that *Ills. 95–105* known as the Royal Cemetery of Ur where up to 74 persons were buried in order to accompany the deceased king. It is significant that the chariot burials which are a feature of the period at Kish and at Ur have also been discovered at Susa in Iran. The practice of sending *Ills. 106–108* retainers to their death with the king has now been noted in a cuneiform tablet entitled 'The Death of Gilgamesh'.

At Ur the Early Dynastic graves are, apart from their

111 A model chariot from Tell Agrab. Although badly corroded, it shows delicate modelling of the heads of the four asses drawing it. The chariot has only two wheels, the solid type with studded rims. The group is also of interest from a technical point of view, being an early example of the *cire perdue* technique of casting bronze

contents, interesting architecturally, for they illustrate the use of stone, of the dome, of corbelling and the barrel vault for the construction of which stone, kiln-fired burnt bricks, as well as mud-bricks were used.

Metallurgy and the fine arts now spread in glorious abundance, much of it immobilized below ground in deference to the extravagant concepts, more congenial to the Egyptian than to the Mesopotamian mind, which demanded every kind of endowment for the deceased king. The abandonment of this uneconomic and no doubt unpopular practice of human sacrifices on a large scale seems to have coincided with a decline in Sumerian authority after 2500 BC.

Ills. 109–113

113 One of the finest and most beautiful examples of Early Dynastic craftsmanship from the Royal Cemetery at Ur is this gold dagger and its sheath. Although other daggers were found, this one surpasses them all. The blade and the sheath are both of solid gold and the blade has a central rib for strength. One side of the sheath, worn outwards from the belt, is decorated with a very rich filigree and exquisite granulated gold work. The openwork design is derived from the woven grass sheaths in which the common people carried their daggers and the reverse side of the sheath is perfectly plain. The hilt is made of a single piece of lapis lazuli which is studded with gold nails.

The dagger was found on a loosely coiled leather belt, or baldric, which had been plated with silver and had a square buckle. An almost completely decayed shell cylinder seal with lapis lazuli caps and a design of fighting animals was found with it. Also hanging from the belt was a toilet set in a gold case which had been cast in one piece and contained a gold ear-scoop, stiletto and tweezers on a silver wire

112 The gold vessels found in some of the Royal Tombs at Ur are superb examples of the goldsmith's craft. In many instances they were beaten from a single sheet of gold. The gold spouted and fluted feeding cup (opposite, above) is elliptical in cross-section and together with the fluted tumbler (below left), was found in the tomb of Queen Shub-ad. The other three vessels came from the tomb of Mes-kalam-shar. The fluted bowl (left) has lugs of lapis lazuli, an engraved chevron design below the rim and a rosette engraved on the base. The fluting has a bold and somewhat unfinished appearance compared to the delicacy of a similar bowl from the tomb of Queen Shub-ad. Above right is a plain bowl, inscribed with the name of Mes-kalam-shar, which was found grasped in the dead man's hands. Below it, a lamp of the usual 'shell' form is similarly inscribed on the base with his name

114–116 The sculpture from Mari is far more sophisticated than, for example, sculpture from Tell Asmar which appears to be relatively provincial and sometimes crudely carved (*cf. Ills. 31, 33, 117*). Examples occur in alabaster and calcite of gods, rulers, priests and temple servants. *Ill. 114* A seated statuette of a woman from Mari apparently wearing a 'polos' on her head, and an overall loose covering cloak. Both garments appear to be peculiar to the Mari region and are unknown elsewhere; *Ill. 115* Gypsum statue of Ikushshamagan, king of Mari, from the Ishtar temple at Mari, *c.* 2900–2685 BC; *Ill. 116* Profile of an alabaster seated statue of Ebikhil, superintendent of the Ishtar temple at Mari, dedicated to the goddess: best quality of Early Dynastic statuary from the site

117, 118   Two views of a formal kneeling statue of a priest or king from the 'square temple' at Tell Asmar of semi-translucent dark amber-coloured alabaster, *c.* 2750 BC, found with a group of votive statuettes, *cf. Ill. 33* bottom right; *Ill. 118* Seated statuette of the singer Urnanshe from the Ishtar temple at Mari, dedicated to the goddess Ishtar and perpetuating him in his role at religious ceremonies. The identification of Akkadian names on Sumerian style statuary at such an early period is of interest as evidence of a movement from the Central Euphrates in the direction of Babylonia where the Sumerians were eventually to be displaced politically by this newer people speaking a Semitic language

Early Dynastic stone statuary rarely reached the high level of metallurgical achievements. At Mari however on the middle Euphrates there are some splendid calcite and

Ills. 114–116, 118 alabaster statues of the gods, rulers and priests, some of them inscribed with Akkadian names. At Tell Asmar we

Ills. 31, 33, 117 are confronted by the work of a provincial workshop, the merits of which have been much exaggerated.

The Sumerian tradition of stone carving both of human and animal figures is well reflected in Iran: at Susa carved plaques, and statuary in the style of Early Dynastic III as well as stone vases, cylinder seals, metal vessels, tools and weapons betray a close relationship with southern Mesopotamia. At Susa again pedestal vases decorated with designs of humped bulls in relief already betray a connection with carvings characteristic of the Indus valley, and we may admit with some confidence that trade relationship with Harappān cities were then ready for development.

Assur

The widespread influence of Sumer at the end of the Early Dynastic period is also well demonstrated far up the river Tigris at the city of Assur which after 2000 BC was to become the religious capital of Assyria. Temple G which is thought to have been dedicated to a goddess, probably Ishtar, was laid out in a simple type of ground plan, with oblong sanctuary and side chambers, as in many other Mesopotamian cities such as Mari and Nuzi. At Assur there were benches against the walls upon which statues in Sumerian form, depicted as clothed in fleecy skins, were dedicated to the god. Models of pedestalled houses, perhaps shrines, decorated with doves and snakes, were also associated. The most remarkable discovery however

Ill. 119 was a painted gypsum plaque apparently depicting the goddess lying on her bed. She was accoutred with jewellery and choker such as were found on Queen Shub-ad and her attendants in the Royal Cemetery of Ur, and was thus unmistakably reminiscent of Sumerian religious practice. The city of Assur would seem to represent the most northerly penetration of direct Sumerian rule at this time (Early Dynastic III) though objects of Sumerian manufacture have been found in even more distant places such as Byblos on the west coast of the Lebanon.

The Agade Period

In about 2370 B C history records the ascent to the throne of the founder of the Agade dynasty, Sargon, who for the first time established political control over a large part of Mesopotamia under a Semitic as opposed to a Sumerian regime; that is to say the language of the rulers was Semitic Akkadian. A bronze head discovered at Nineveh, *Ill. 74* already mentioned, perhaps depicts that monarch himself. In style the hairdressing is closely comparable with a slightly earlier electrum helmet which belonged to Mes- *Ill. 122* kalam-shar, a prince buried with a rich panoply of funeral deposits and offerings in one of the latest Early Dynastic graves at Ur.

Sargon and his successors took over their Sumerian heritage and earned their acquisitions both by the might of arms and by their high development of the arts. Statuary and seals of the period may be ranked amongst the finest monuments ever produced on Mesopotamian soil. The great stele of Naram-Sin, fourth monarch of the *Ill. 121* dynasty, illustrates his victory over a west Iranian chief and is a notable artistic achievement. The king is depicted leading his warriors to the top of a high, wooded mountain: an impression of movement, soft and easy flow of line, cleverly contrived spacing and bold sense of composition are characteristic of the period. This monument is executed in the grand manner and can be matched

119 A fragment of a painted gypsum plaque from Assur shows the goddess Ishtar lying on her bed. The jewellery and choker which she wears is unmistakably reminiscent of that found upon the bodies of Queen Shub-ad and her attendants in the great death-pit at Ur. This is part of the evidence which shows that Sumerian religious beliefs and practices were being carried as far north as Assur in the Early Dynastic III period

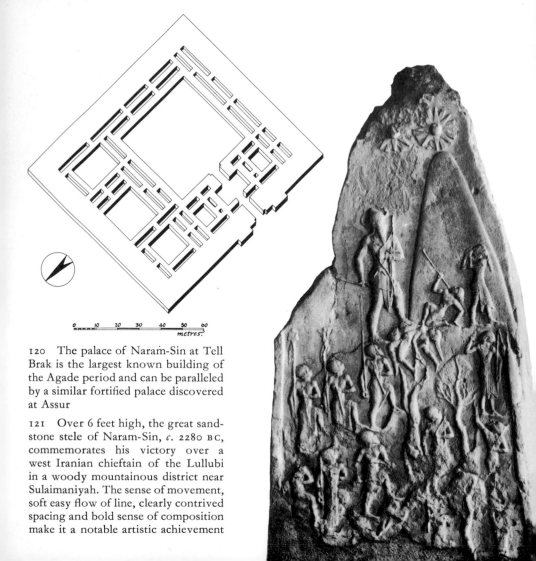

0 10 20 30 40 50 60
metres.

120 The palace of Naram-Sin at Tell Brak is the largest known building of the Agade period and can be paralleled by a similar fortified palace discovered at Assur

121 Over 6 feet high, the great sandstone stele of Naram-Sin, c. 2280 BC, commemorates his victory over a west Iranian chieftain of the Lullubi in a woody mountainous district near Sulaimaniyah. The sense of movement, soft easy flow of line, clearly contrived spacing and bold sense of composition make it a notable artistic achievement

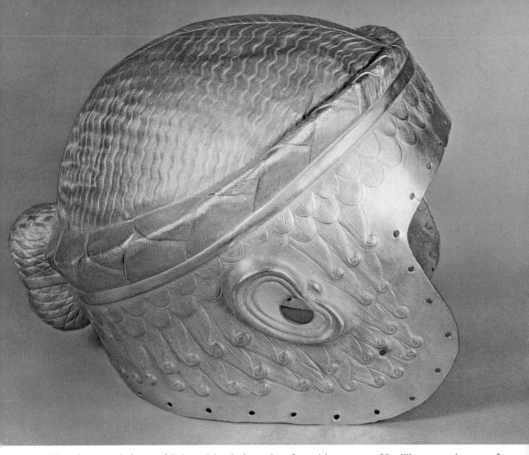

122 The electrum helmet of Prince Mes-kalam-shar from his grave at Ur. The grave is one of the latest of those in the Royal Cemetery and dates from *c*. 2500 BC. The gold is 15 carat (electrum being a natural alloy of gold and silver) and the entire helmet was hammered from a single sheet of metal. Features such as the ears and the knot of hair are in relief (*cf. Ill. 74*) and the details of the hair chased

in miniature by the superbly carved cylinder seals which are another and no less brilliant achievement.

The largest known building of the Agade period is a palace discovered at Tell Brak in the Habur region of north Syria with a frontage of over 100 metres. The inscribed bricks record the names of the same king, Naram-Sin, who clearly established it as a fortress and blockhouse to guard his lines of communication with Anatolia where, as we know from much later texts, his ancestor Sargon had promoted trade and supported merchants who had appealed to him for help. No doubt

Ill. 120

109

123 The huge white limestone stele of Ur Nammu – 10 feet high and 5 feet wide – records the conferment of kingship by the gods. This is a concept stemming from the earliest times, since texts mention that after the Flood kingship descended again from upon high. Here we have a relatively late example of the divine right of kings dated *c*. 2100 BC. At the top the sun and a crescent moon are suspended above a figure of the king, larger than any of the other human figures depicted. The king salutes a seated goddess who has a child sitting on her lap, the feet may be discerned on the side of the throne. The goddess, now fragmentary, is probably Nin-gal and in her attitude she is symbolic of the king's divine origins. Above streams of flowing water pour down.

The second register shows the king twice in two separate scenes. On the right he is introduced to the moon god Nanna who invests him with the symbols of justice and right, the mason's chief implements: the rod and the line. The scene to the left shows him saluting the goddess Nin-gal seated on a throne-stool. The lower part of the stele has been very badly damaged, a fragment of the next row shows the king, assisted by an attendant, carrying building instruments, an axe and an adze

the motive for his interest in north Syria was to secure the rich metal ores of eastern Asia Minor. It can hardly be a coincidence that contemporary metal work discovered in treasure troves at Brak can in part match the treasure found in the second city of Troy which during the Agade period must have been in touch, probably by the sea route, with the cities of north Syria and Mesopotamia.

Ur

The capital city of the dynasty, Agade itself, has yet to be found, probably in the neighbourhood of Babylon, and a great prize may await its discoverer. The dynasty was brought to an end by barbarous hordes called the Guti who reflect the relative backwardness of western Iranian mountaineers at the time. There was however one more brilliant Neo-Sumerian revival, first at Lagash under Gudea whose black diorite statues and long Sumerian inscriptions record another period of prosperity. But the

Ill. 124

124 One of the finest statues of the Sumerian revival shows Gudea, King of Lagash, or possibly his son Ur-Ningirsu standing in quiet contemplation. The inscription has been partly broken away and effaced probably when the city was sacked

125–128   The ziggurat of Ur still stands high above the excavations of the city with the spoil heaps radiating out from them into the desert. The ramps which supported the staircases rising up to the temple on the top of the ziggurat can be clearly seen in the view (*Ill. 126*) taken during the actual excavations when the great courtyard and temple built within the sacred enclosure at

the foot of the building were found. 'Weeper' holes in the burnt-brick casing (*Ill. 127*, from the south-west) must have been designed to prevent the massive mud-brick core from splitting when it became saturated with water during the rainy season. *Ill. 128* is a reconstructed view of the ziggurat as it probably looked under the Third Dynasty

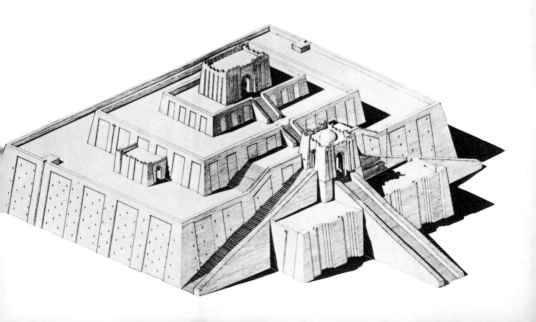

129 The great period of sculpture during the Sumerian revival, elsewhere best represented by the workshops at Lagash, is illustrated also by this vigorous carving of a woman's head in diorite. The engraved modulations of the hair, elaborate bun at the back of the head, and fillet around the forehead are an admirable setting for the face. The head, which may be dated to *c*. 2150 BC, was found in the Nin-Gal temple at Ur

Ill. 123

Ills. 125–128

Ills. 129, 131

Ill. 130

climax of this period of revival was achieved by the Third Dynasty of Ur whose first two rulers, Ur Nammu and Shulgi, made Ur and Uruk glorious cities, rebuilt the sacred enclosure, the *temenos*, and wherever possible substituted kiln-fired burnt-bricks of the finest quality for the traditional mud-brick which so frequently required repair. The noblest monument of the time is the great Ziggurat of Ur, a staged tower approached by triple staircases. The monarchs of this dynasty also established direct authority over Assur and were supreme at Susa in Iran where some rich treasures, statuary and jewellery of gold and other metals, were deposited by them.

The authority of the Neo-Sumerian dynasty of Ur even so far north as Assyria is well exemplified by the Ishtar Temple E, conventional in plan, approached by a stepped

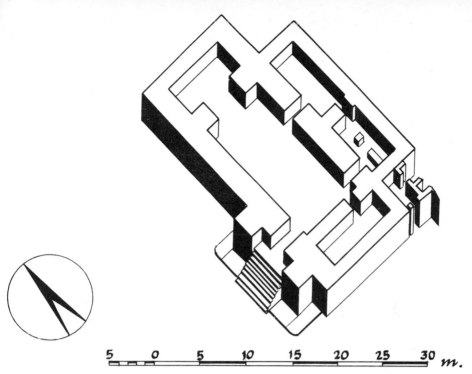

130 The influence of Sumerian architecture in Assyria is apparent in the plan of Temple E at Assur, dedicated to the goddess Ishtar. It was built by Zariqu, viceroy of Bur-Sin the third king of the Third Dynasty of Ur, 2037–2028 BC

entrance flanked by towers, laid out with oblong sanctuary, a room at each end and two others to one side; the corners of the building face approximately the cardinal points of the compass. A votive plaque recorded that the temple was erected by one Zariqu who proclaimed himself viceroy of Amar-Suen (once known as Bur-Sin) the third king of the Third Dynasty of Ur (2037–2028 BC). At Assur graves of this period were sometimes lavishly endowed with offerings, and one of them which contained a gold frontlet impressed with concentric circles, gold lunate earrings, etched carnelian beads and a lapis lazuli seal in the Cappadocian style, is of particular interest. The quality of its jewellery is to some extent comparable to rich deposits found at Tepe Hissar in northern Iran, in the last period of its occupation (IIIB and IIIC), with a

131 A copper goddess dating from *c.* 2100–2000 BC found in a wooden box which had formed the base for a limestone statue. Also found with her was a whetstone, the group may have been a craftsman's dedication. She has the horns of divinity, and wears metal rings round her neck. Her long tresses fall below her shoulders and her dress is flounced and pleated. Her arms, made separately, are now missing

likely date, as we shall see, of about 2000 BC. Elsewhere in Sumer, at Uruk, there is also similar evidence in the shape of a magnificent collar composed of carnelian, gold filigree surrounding agate, silver and turquoise beads, all threaded on silver wires. The turquoise was no doubt imported from Iran. This set of jewellery was made for a priestess of Shu Sin, the King of Ur (2028–2003 BC); such ornaments would not have been out of place at Hissar.

CHAPTER SIX

Tepe Hissar III
and the New Dynasties of Babylonia

Since much material associated with the Third Dynasty of Ur appears to be comparable with discoveries in northern Iran it is interesting that we are at last able to point to an Iranian building which has some analogies to one in Mesopotamia. We have noticed above the plan of a temple dedicated to Ishtar at Assur, and with this we may compare that of the 'Burnt Building' at Tepe Hissar IIIB. *Ill. 132* Both are oblong buildings with a single entrance defended by towers; each is divided into three parts with a store-room at one end and flanking chambers. Moreover the lengths, though not the proportions, of the two buildings are approximately similar: about 26 metres at Hissar, 29 metres at Assur. It is possible, though not certain, that the end room at Hissar contained a shrine within it. At all events here for the first time we have two architectural units in Iraq and Iran which, however remotely, may be the result of a common technological development at a time when the two countries were increasingly in touch with one another. We need not press the similarity too closely, but it would not be surprising if the two buildings had been built not very far apart in time, for as we shall see at Hissar, this was a period of great prosperity and that must have been largely due to a transcontinental trade.

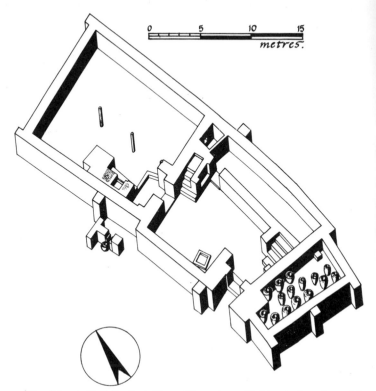

132   The 'Burnt Building' at Tepe Hissar has affinities in its plan with
the Ishtar Temple at Assur (*Ill. 130*) and similarly may reflect Sumerian
architectural influence in Iran

The mud-brick building at Hissar was richly endowed
with gold daggers, gold, silver and copper vessels and
expensive jewellery; millet was found in the store-rooms.
The place fell in dramatic circumstances to enemy attack.
Signs of a desperate battle were evident from many ovate
flint arrowheads in the precincts of the building which was
finally devastated by fire. About a dozen charred skeletons
of men, women and children were found within it.
Communal graves elsewhere on the site may have been
the result of defeat at the hands of more powerful cities
on the other side of the mountains, Shah Tepe or Tureng
Tepe for instance, where later traces of occupation appear.

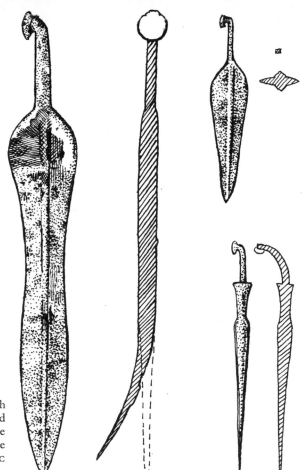

133 The types of spears with medial ribs and ridge-stopped tangs found at Tepe Hissar are important typological evidence to suggest a date of *c*. 2000 BC as a date for its last phases

In the last phases of its lifetime (III B and C), Tepe Hissar seems to have been an extremely rich centre, well equipped with all those kinds of goods which were coveted as the fruits of civilization. Apart from an abundance of gold, variegated jewellery, copper and silver vessels, there were alabaster, calcite and veined stone vases of exceptional beauty and elegance. Pedestal vases in stone were much favoured. There were many varieties of beads, among them much lapis lazuli, and it may well be that Hissar was an entrepôt in the profitable trade which must have resulted through the export of that stone from the mines of Badakhshan to other parts of Iran as well as to

Ill. 135

135 A selection of gold hair ornaments and necklaces of agate and carnelian beads found at Tepe Hissar and dated to *c.* 2000 BC. Hissar was an important centre on the caravan routes and such finds illustrate the luxury trade in expensive goods which were coveted as the fruits of civilization

134   The combination of the basic forms of an axe and an adze produced a single simple and useful tool, the axe-adze. One of the earliest examples of the type is this specimen which was found in the 'Burnt Building' at Tepe Hissar

Mesopotamia. There is sufficient continuity of style between the objects of the last two periods of Hissar III B–C to make it certain that both were in a continuous development, not separated by any length of time. But in spite of the great variety of material goods it is still impossible to be certain about the exact date of these Iranian phases of civilization owing to the absence of written records which may yet of course be found.

On the basis of developments in style and in technology dates have been proposed by various authorities, some as early as 2300 BC, others as late as 1500 BC. None has used convincing arguments. Since many of the metal and stone vessels, as well as the weapons, are in the Early Dynastic tradition of the Royal Cemetery of Ur there is a case for arguing the earlier of the two dates mentioned. The case for proposing a date some time after 2000 BC depends largely on the use of the axe-adze and of certain types of well developed spears with medial rib and ridge-stopped tangs. But in fact there are parallels for the latter from Carchemish and Ugarit in north Syria which may well be dated at least a century before 2000 BC, and Hissar is situated geographically in just the region where one would expect smiths to adapt and combine axe and adze to form a single tool. There are excellent parallels for this

Ill. 133

Ill. 134

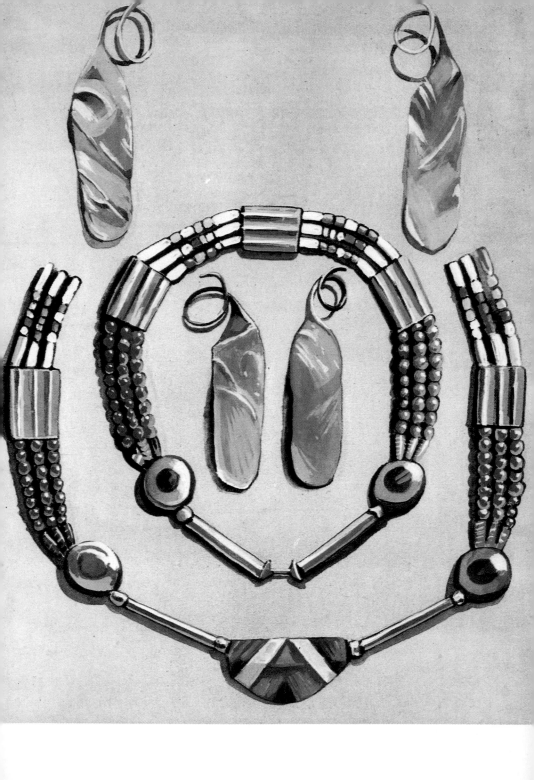

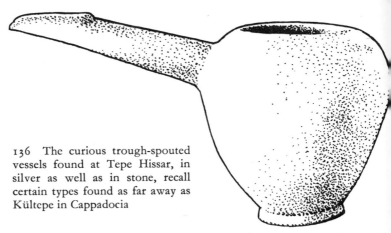

136 The curious trough-spouted vessels found at Tepe Hissar, in silver as well as in stone, recall certain types found as far away as Kültepe in Cappadocia

rather rare type of instrument as late as the reign of Shalmaneser III, *c.* 850 BC, but that alone would be an inadequate reason for arguing that this instrument was unknown in Assyria where it had not yet appeared in an earlier context before that time.

In the absence of conclusive evidence there are in fact stronger reasons for dating Hissar IIIB a little before 2000 BC and IIIC a little after it, or indeed at about that time. In general the extravagantly long-spouted, sometimes trough-spouted vessels from Hissar, in silver as well as in stone, recall certain types used in the *karum* at Kültepe in Cappadocia, as also do stone vessels decorated with concentric circles which can be compared with others used at Susa during the Third Dynasty of Ur. The latter is a period which can also offer parallels for the many types of elaborately decorated copper mace-heads that are also a feature of Hissar III. Lastly the use of lead vessels is also suggestive of the interest in that commodity at Kültepe *c.* 1900 BC, whilst the modelling of faience amulets, including frogs, at Shah Tepe which appears to have outlived Hissar affords parallels with the Larşa period in Mesopotamia at approximately the same date.

There is other evidence to illustrate the widespread contact between Hissar and distant cities at this period.

Ill. 136

Ill. 138

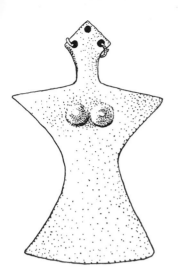

137 A stylized alabaster mother-goddess figurine from Tepe Hissar III with copper rings threaded through the head

138 Elaborately decorated copper mace-heads are a feature of Tepe Hissar III, such as this example surmounted by a copper animal

Certain types of compartmented copper seals have been found here, at Shahi Tump in Baluchistan, at Anau III in Turkestan, and one decorated with an eagle can be matched at Susa. The alleged presence of amber may imply an even more distant trade and one cylinder seal carries the design of an Indian humped bull.

Finally it is worthy of notice that in Hissar IIIB the skull of a horse was found and furthermore the horse is alleged to have been domesticated at Shah Tepe much earlier still, thus long anticipating the first appearance of it at Boghazköy in Central Asia Minor in the early Hittite period. An analysis of some 250 skeletal remains in Hissar III revealed the fact that females to males were in the ratio of two to one and that 87 per cent of the persons examined had died before the age of 40, a very sharp contrast to modern average figures for longevity in America and in Europe.

The extraordinary wealth accumulated from trans-Caspian trade is also most strikingly shown by a celebrated hoard known as the Asterabad Treasure which included gold, metal vessels, a gold ibex head, axe-adzes, copper spears and other implements. Amongst them two golden signal horns or trumpets closely matched similar instruments from Hissar IIIC and were obviously contemporary.

Ill. 140

Ill. 139

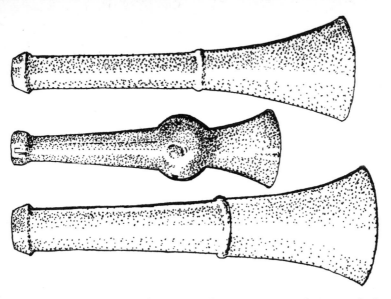

139, 140   Silver trumpets from Tepe Hissar. The centre one is very similar to the golden signal trumpet from the Asterabad Treasure (*Ill. 140* opposite). The Treasure, now lost, is a striking example of the wealth of the Caspian trade. It included objects in both precious and base metals and various types of implements

The Rise of New Empires

The widespread contact between distant parts of the civilized world at that time implied a desire to share in the wealth available to man, and a determination to compete for it if it were withheld. It is no surprise that in about 2000 BC, after a millennium and a half of Sumerian dominance in Mesopotamia, new forces both there and in Iran were ready to take over the authority of government.

We have already seen that the monarchs of Agade had assumed authority in the twenty-fourth century BC, and in so doing had for the first time established rule by speakers of a Semitic language. In due course they were supplanted by the Third Dynasty of Ur, the last Sumerian line of rulers, whose last king Ibbi-Suen in about 2000 BC was carried captive to Iran. Afterwards, although the Sumerian language was long used by learned scribes for religious and magical literature, the Sumerians themselves ceased to be important. Their great heritage was however

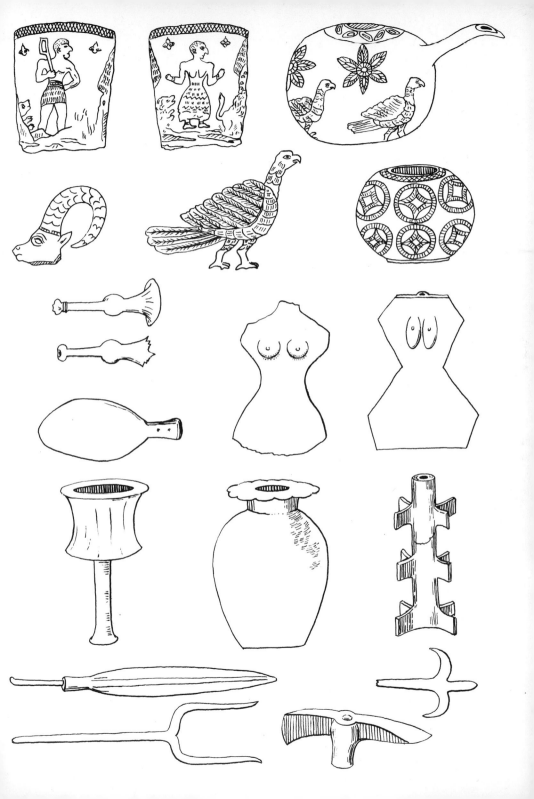

taken over and organized by new Semitic dynasties, Amorites and others, who swarmed eastwards across Syria into the fertile valleys of Tigris and Euphrates. New capitals aspired to imperial control: first Isin, then Larsa, then Babylon, occasionally admitting elements from western Iran within the government. In about

Ills. 141, 142

141, 142 A terracotta plaque of a nude, bearded hero, with curled hair and moustache illustrates the work of the later Ur craftsmen of *c.* 2100 B C. The hero carries a vase from which
streams of water flow on either side. The terracotta plaque (*Ill. 142*) shows a woman musician
playing the cymbals and dates from the Sumerian revival *c.* 2000 B C. She wears her hair in long
curled tresses and her upper garment, cut in the style of a bolero, has a raised decoration

2000 B C we may discern a turning point between these
newer forces and the old; it was a period at which
Mesopotamia was reorganizing itself and Iran was await-
ing the emergence of a vigorous agricultural tribe, the
Kassites, who were later on to play a powerful part on the
Near Eastern stage.

MAP OF MESOPOTAMIA AND IRAN

Scale at 28° latitude

Miles

0   100   200   300   400   500

0   100   200   300   400   500   600   700   800

Kilometres

Contours at 2,000 metres

Bibliography

The most recent information on discoveries is to be found in the periodical literature and the following periodicals contain some of the source material for this book:

IRAN   Journal of the British Institute of Persian Studies, 1963–
IRANICA ANTIQUA, 1962–
IRAQ   Journal of the British School of Archaeology, Iraq, 1934–
   See particularly Vol. XXIV (1960). *Ur in Retrospect*, edited by Mallowan and Wiseman
MÉMOIRES DE LA MISSION ARCHÉOLOGIQUE EN PERSE, 1900–
SUMER   Published by the Iraq Antiquities Department, 1945–
SYRIA   Published by L'Institut Français d'Archéologie de Beyrouth, 1920–

ANDRAE, W.   *Das Wiedererstandene Assur*, Berlin, 1938
ARNE, T. A. J.   *Excavations at Shah Tepe, Iran*, Stockholm, 1945
CHILDE, V. G.   *New Light on the Most Ancient East*, London, 1952
CONTENAU, G.   *Manuel d'Archéologie Mesopotamienne*, I–IV, Paris, 1927–47
DELOUGAZ, P.   *Pottery from the Diyala Region*, Oriental Institute, Chicago, 1952
DELOUGAZ, P. and LLOYD, S.   *Pre-Sargonid Temples in the Diyala Region*, Oriental Institute, Chicago, 1942
DRIVER, G. R.   *Semitic Writing*, 1944, rev. ed., London, 1954
FALKENSTEIN, A.   *Archaische Texte aus Uruk*, Berlin, 1936
FRANKFORT, H.   *Art and Architecture of the Ancient Orient*, rev. ed., London, 1958
GHIRSHMAN, R.   *Iran*, London, 1954
HEINRICH, E.   (ed.) *Vorläufiger Bericht über Uruk-Warka*, I–XIV, Berlin, 1929–59
                 Kleinfunde aus den Archaischen Tempelschichten in Uruk, Berlin, 1936
JACOBSEN, T.   *The Sumerian King List*, Oriental Institute, Chicago, 1939
KRAMER, S. N.   *Sumerian Mythology*, Philadelphia, 1944
                 History Begins at Sumer, London, 1958
                 The Sumerians, Chicago, 1963
LABAT, R.   *Manuel d'Epigraphie Akkadienne*, Paris, 1948
LE BRETON, A.   'The Early Periods at Susa' in *Iraq*, XIX (1957), p. 79
LLOYD, S.   *Art of the Ancient Near East*, London, 1961
MALLOWAN, M. E. L.   *Twenty-Five Years of Mesopotamian Discovery*, 2nd ed., London, 1959
PARROT, A.   *Archéologie Mesopotamienne*, 2 vols., Paris, 1946, 1953
                 Sumer, London, 1960
PERKINS, A. L.   *The Comparative Archaeology of Early Mesopotamia*, Chicago, 1949
POPE, A. U.   *A Survey of Persian Art*, 4 vols., London, 1938
SCHMIDT, E. F.   *Excavations at Tepe Hissar, Dangham*, Philadelphia, 1937
SPEISER, E. A.   *Excavations at Tepe Gawra*, I, Philadelphia, 1935
TOBLER, A. J.   *Excavations at Tepe Gawra*, II, Philadelphia, 1950
WISEMAN, D. J.   *Cylinder Seals of Western Asia*, London [1959]
WOOLLEY, C. L.   *Excavations at Ur: a Record of Twelve Years' Work*, London, 1954
                 Ur Excavations:
                 II, *The Royal Cemetery*, London, 1934
                 IV, *The Early Periods*, London, 1956
                 V, *The Ziggurat and its Surroundings*, London, 1939

List of Illustrations

The author and publishers are grateful to the many official bodies, institutions and individuals mentioned below for their assistance in supplying original illustration material. Illustrations without acknowledgement are from originals in Thames & Hudson's archives.

Chronological table of some major Mesopotamian sites.

Museum, Baghdad. Photo courtesy
Directorate General of Antiquities,
Iraq

52 Limestone trough from Uruk. British
Museum. Photo John Freeman

53 Sculptured alabaster vase from Uruk.
Iraq Museum, Baghdad. Photo
courtesy Directorate General of
Antiquities, Iraq

54, 55 Two Jemdet Nasr period account
tablets. British Museum. Photo courtesy of the Trustees of the British
Museum

56 Development of the *bucranium* design
on Halaf pots from Chagar Bazar.
After Mallowan

57 Stone libation jug with mosaic inlay
from Uruk. Iraq Museum, Baghdad.
Photo Max Hirmer

58 Stone bowl from Sin Temple IV,
Khafajah, with mother-of-pearl in-
lays. Iraq Museum, Baghdad. Photo
Max Hirmer

59 Pottery scraper from the Royal
Cemetery at Ur. British Museum.
Photo courtesy of the Trustees of the
British Museum

60, 61 The Blau Monuments; shale plaque,
obverse and reverse. British Museum.
Photos John Freeman

62 Copper chisel from the Royal
Cemetery at Ur. British Museum.
Photo courtesy of the Trustees of the
British Museum

63, 64 The Blau Monuments; pointed shale
tool, obverse and reverse. British
Museum. Photos John Freeman

65 Foundation tablet of A-an-ne-pad-da,
King of Ur, *c.* 2600 BC. British
Museum. Photo courtesy of the
Trustees of the British Museum

66 Foundation brick of Enanatum I,
c. 2450 BC. British Museum. Photo
Peter Clayton

67 Foundation tablet of Eannatum,
King of Lagash, *c.* 2500 BC. British
Museum. Photo courtesy of the
Trustees of the British Museum

68 Clay stamp of Naram-Sin and impression, *c.* 2280 BC. British Museum.
Photo Peter Clayton

69 Foundation tablet of Ur Nammu, *c.*
2110 BC. British Museum. Photo
courtesy of the Trustees of the
British Museum

70 Uninscribed clay tablet. British
Museum. Photo Peter Clayton

71 Cylinder seal impression, Jemdet
Nasr period, from Khafajah. Photo
Oriental Institute, University of
Chicago

72 Cylinder seal with running goats,
c. 2800 BC. British Museum. Photo
courtesy of the Trustees of the
British Museum

73 Cylinder seal with bearded heroes,
aragonite, *c.* 2300 BC. British
Museum. Photo courtesy of the
Trustees of the British Museum

74 Cast bronze head of Sargon of
Agade (?) from Nineveh. Iraq
Museum, Baghdad. Photo Max
Hirmer

75–82 Cylinder seals and impressions, Uruk
to Isin-Larsa periods.
75 Uruk-Jemdet Nasr, limestone; 76
Jemdet Nasr, gypsum; 77 E.D.I.,
limestone; 78 Agade period, green-
stone; 79 Ur III, black haematite;
80 Ur III, green schist; 81 Isin-
Larsa, black haematite; 82 Isin-Larsa,
black haematite. British Museum.
Photos John Freeman

Index

Numbers in italics refer to illustrations